GW01444929

Turning The Tables: The Story of Extrer

ECW was the upstart promotion that revolutionised the wrestling industry. Turning The Tables is the first published history of the company that grew from a run-down bingo hall to become a national pay-per-view competitor... then crashed in a sea of debt.

John Lister gives an independent, objective and informative account that reveals hidden secrets and shatters common myths. From a little-known truth about ECW's most famous feud to a blow-by-blow account of what really happened in Revere, this book will give you the true story behind America's most controversial wrestling group.

(**www.turningthetables.co.uk**)

■■

Slamthology: Collected Wrestling Writings 1991-2004

John Lister is one of Britain's most respected wrestling journalists. Mixing travelogue, humour, fiction, history and opinion, this collection brings together the best of his work from the past fourteen years.

The first section of this book features three epic accounts of voyages to see wrestling in the United States, from the ECW Arena to the Dallas Sportatorium by way of WWF pay-per-views and Memphis television.

The second section comprises more than 40 articles, some previously unpublished, including histories of British and American wrestling, the statistics behind WCW's collapse, and a disgraceful allegation about Tommy Rich.

(www.slamthology.co.uk)

Purodyssey

A Tokyo Wrestling Diary

By John Lister

Notes

Unlike my previous travel journals (which were reproduced in Slamthology), I've not gone into extensive detail about every match I saw in Japan. This is partly because there were far more than on any previous trip I've taken and partly because I see so many shows these days that it's sometimes hard to remember individual bouts. However, for the sake of being complete, I have included the full results at the end of the book.

Rather than include photographs in the book, which would likely have bumped up the price and risked being poor quality (and monochrome), I've put together a full online gallery which you can access at www.johnlisterwriting.com/purodyssey.html

Introduction

A quarter of a century ago I read a magazine article that changed my life. Eventually.

As a 15-year-old who'd been a wrestling fan for just a couple of years, I read a Sports Review Wrestling article titled "Are you a real wrestling fan? Grade yourself with our 38-point checklist." Some I had already done: "Sit front row at an independent match" or "See a videotape of Gorgeous George." Others I would later achieve: "Attend a wrestling fans' convention" or "Go to a costume party dressed as a wrestler." (The Million Dollar Man. One person recognised it.)

Some more are still works in progress such as "Follow a wrestler's career from rookie debut to world champion." I saw Gary Steele's first match on video and then saw him win the NWA title live, while I saw Jack Gallagher's first match in person and, well, let's just keep an eye on 205 Live.

But one challenge would elude me for most of my life: "Attend seven cards in seven nights."

Those of you who've read my previous travel journals will know I made a couple of attempts Stateside back in 1997. In February I fell at the first hurdle when it turned out the weekly USWA Memphis house show was cancelled. Seven months later I'd racked up five shows (four of them before I even went to bed for the first time on the trip) when a USWA cancellation let me down again, this time in Louisville. After that trip, life got in the way and, though I made several more trips to the US, I never again attempted the septuple.

There was always Japan of course. I knew of people who'd visited, but it seemed impossibly complicated to organize, plus the glory days appeared to be over. But come the mid-2010s I saw more and more people doing it, using the Internet not just to plan the visit, but to update people in real time about their progress. Then in August 2017 I saw Twitter user @mortenvh posting so enthusiastically about his first visit to the country that within a matter of moments I had a flight and hotel reservation and a considerably increased credit card bill.

It was time.

Friday 29th December 2017

Any pretence that I was doing something unique by flying to Tokyo for wrestling was out the window when I spotted a fellow passenger in the departure lounge wearing a Bullet Club shirt. Little did I know just how far from rare the sight of a fellow Westerner was to become.

Despite arriving nearly four hours early for the flight (WifeBus doesn't offer a selection of schedules), a wander round the terminal and a somewhat ironically chosen sushi lunch meant the time flew by and I was suddenly on a plane ready to depart. That's more that can be said for the in-flight entertainment system, which was refusing to work, leading to us sitting on the ground for an hour and forty minutes after our scheduled departure time as British Airways desperately tried to avoid spending 12 hours with a couple of hundred people bored out of their skulls.

Eventually the crew had to settle for broadcast mode, a disappointment that showed just how technology has changed since those late-90s trips. Instead of a selection of hundreds of on-demand programs, we now "only" had a dozen or so channels of films and TV shows that each played on a loop, meaning you had to flick through and hope you found one that was near the beginning. I certainly felt my age thinking back to the days when you had to stare at a single screen in the aisle and your choice was Fly Away Home or nothing.

It's surprising how easy it is to adjust to such a long flight: two films and lunch and I was already at the point when I could reframe "there's still six hours to go" as "we're already most of the way there." This process wasn't helped by the in-flight map, however, which for several hours over Siberia showed no landmarks or terrain variations at any of the available map scales. It's somewhat chilling to realise that if the plane made an emergency landing here, you'd probably be waiting days if not weeks to be rescued.

Arriving at the airport in Tokyo, I'd expected to be overwhelmed by the sheer 'Japaneseness' of it all, but the presence of widespread English language signs and the globally familiar look of airports meant it just felt like a normal arrivals experience that just happened to have a lot of Japanese faces and some unusual symbols. Oh, and a newsagent that not only had the expected weekly wrestling magazines, but also a dedicated Los Ingobernables Japan publication.

Of course, there's one aspect of arriving at an airport that truly defines entering a foreign culture: the toilets. Back in 1996, the first sign that I was actually in America was when I went into the cubicle and saw the bowl already near-full of water, something that in the UK would be an indication that something had gone horrifically wrong.

Here every stereotype I had about Japan was justified with what proved to be a standard feature: a control panel that not only included buttons for spray-cleaning your backside after doing your business (an experience that is… not unpleasant) but also the option to disguise the sound of your ablutions with a recording of running water. Later in the week I'd find models that even had a button to activate some sort of odour-removing technology. There was an inherent design flaw however: with no drying mechanism, you are left to take care of your freshly rinsed area with Japanese toilet paper, which has all the strength and water-resistance of sherbet.

As I was arriving several hours before my check-in (and as it was now around 2am UK time), I'd originally planned to start my cliché bingo card with a couple of hours in a capsule hotel. The delay made that unnecessary, so I got to work on the admin, attempting to buy some wrestling tickets at a ticket agency desk (failing because the on-sale period had ended) and picking up a local SIM card that had been delivered to me at the airport post office.

It was then time to take the train in to the city and get my next demonstration of Japanese efficiency. Not only was I able to buy a ticket (with seat reservation) from a vending machine and make my way to the platform in under three minutes, but the platform had markings to show exactly where to stand to be in line with the nearest carriage door to my seat. Even if a British railway company had the foresight to attempt this, it would no doubt fail because they had no idea how many carriages would be in the train that day. (Unless it's Bristol to Cardiff at 5pm on a weekday when, despite the demand seeming obvious, the answer is always a mere three.)

The train's on-board TV had news coverage where it appeared the main story was that two sets of Japanese businessmen in suits had sat on opposite sides of a table and stared at each other, though there was also a shot of the government's cabinet. It's always good to be reminded that whereas Britain had a spoof documentary about the bureaucratic failures of its Olympics preparations, the Tokyo 2020 equivalent would just be Hiroshi Hase saying "Don't worry. I've got this."

Staring out of the window instead, I had my first true moment of disorientation and a realisation that what's most unsettling about experiencing Japan is not how different it is, but how much of it is so close to the familiar that the tiny differences really throw you. Coming in from Narita Airport, once you've been through a few miles of woodland, the scenery becomes identical to a US city's suburbs except for the curved roofs on buildings. Similarly, busy traffic on city centre roads is utterly familiar and yet slightly unsettling because of the way vans are shaped with more right angles and fewer curves.

Once I arrived at Tokyo Station itself, I went through 20 minutes or so of proper culture shock. While many people describe Tokyo as overwhelming and confusing, I suspect this is much less to do with the city and country itself and far more to do with the fact that it's a massive city and when you get there you're likely jetlagged and dragging luggage around.

My wandering round in circles was mainly because I was under the impression I could simply buy a Suica card (a pre-paid transport smartcard similar to an Oyster card) from a vending machine. It turned out I had to buy it over the counter at a newsstand kiosk where my attempts at basic Japanese proved twice as successful as I had expected. By which I mean I bought two cards instead of one.

After getting my bearings, it was a simple enough subway journey to Suidobashi, the district that's home to the Tokyo Dome and Korakuen Hall. Not only are the subway routes easy to navigate, with a colour for every line and a number for every station, but when changing lines the signs even tell you how many metres you have left to walk to the relevant platform. (If that number increases, you know you've gone wrong.)

There was still a little time left till I could check-in, so I decided the fact was carrying a suitcase was no reason not to walk through Tokyo Dome City, an area that was swarming with people coming out of a convention for the Ultraman TV show and teenage girls waiting to see Hey! Say! JUMP. At the time I described this as the Japanese version of One Direction, though Wikipedia gives this wonderful description of just how gloriously manufactured the whole thing is (and how similar it is to a Japanese wrestling stable or promotion):

Hey! Say! JUMP is a nine-member Japanese all-male band under the Japanese talent agency, Johnny & Associates. The name Hey! Say! refers to the fact that all the members were born in the Heisei period, and JUMP is an acronym for Johnny's Ultra Music Power. The group is split into two sub-groups: Hey! Say! BEST (Boys Excellent Select Team) and Hey! Say! 7 (not to be confused with the temporary group with the same name). The sub-groups consist of the five oldest members (BEST) and four youngest members respectively.

I was to become extremely familiar with the popularity of the group as it was appearing for four straight nights and, not accounting for people who came more than once, I likely saw around a quarter of a million of their fans. It's quite the reminder of just how big subculture can be today to have these shows followed by the New Japan event, with both audiences likely knowing little or anything of the other group's fandom.

With the ticket agency route having failed, I took the opportunity to visit the Korakuen Hall box office where I found a group of people hanging around. Being English (and too dazed to enquire further), I stood behind them and waited my turn. This got a bit confusing when a woman in a tracksuit who was clearly a wrestling promoter ordered everyone to stand in line. (I believe this was former wrestler GAMI.)

It wasn't until she started marching us off down a corridor that I realised I'd inadvertently joined a (presumably ticketed) meet and greet session for the WAVE promotion and, not wanting to risk causing a scene, waiting until they turned the corner and quickly peeled away.

Now I knew I could just walk into the box office area, buying the tickets proved straightforward enough as I simply showed them a printout of the two shows I wanted to attend and then they showed me a seating plan and pointed to a section marked in highlighter pen.

I say "simply", though what actually happened was they pointed to the section and I nodded, then they pointed and looked at me, so I nodded and smiled, then they pointed and looked at me like an idiot, and eventually I realised they wanted me to point to the specific seat I'd like to buy. As I'll note in the guide section at the end of this book, overcoming the language barrier is remarkably simple as long as you aren't bothered by the thought that people might think you are a moron.

Walking over to the hotel I then spotted a 7-11 convenience store, which gave me a chance to pick up an All Japan ticket that I'd bought on line. This proved a little confusing when, rather than a ticket being printed on demand as I'd expected, the staff simply retrieved a pre-printed ticket with an assigned seat from a filing cabinet. As I was able to pick up a ticket from any 7-11 in Tokyo, I'm still not entirely sure how this works. The company website lists 2,600 stores in Tokyo, so even if every store only has one ticket in stock, that's far more seats than are in the venue, and that's before you even get to other retailers and the venue box office. As with so much of Tokyo, it seems the moral is that often it's best not to ask questions when something just seems to work.

I finally made my way to the Wing Korakuen hotel, my choice of which was 45 percent down to price, 45 percent down to being located right across the street from the Tokyo Dome complex, and 10 percent down to the name making me think I'd see Mr Pogo set somebody on fire in the lobby. That wasn't to be, but I did get a warm welcome complete with a small cup of (Japanese) tea and a warm towel at reception.

I tried to play my part but was thrown a little when the woman on the reception desk spoke perfectly understandable English only to giggle after every sentence. While it was initially charming, when I realised it would be a constant, I soon had a facial expression replicating that of Alan Partridge when he was trapped in the lift with the similarly chucklesome Kevin Eldon character. Still, I too was soon showing delight when I discovered the reception area had a 24/7 free-to-use hot drinks facility that included several British tea blends. Yes, there's fitting in with the local culture, but civilised humanity also counts for something. (I was even more grateful for this when I found a grocery store charging just under ten pounds for a box of Yorkshire Tea.)

My room turned out to be big enough to house a fridge and a kettle so large it must have been the matching half of a set with the Samovar trophy that Davey Boy Smith won at the Royal Albert Hall, but small enough that the only place I could actually open my suitcase was on the bed. I stuck around just long enough to check out the TV channel selection. Unlike 20 years ago, quantity of channels is no longer a novelty for British tourists, and quality was not exactly on offer. It turns out every cliché you used to see on Tarrant On TV is based in truth, with at least three channels showing some form of exceptionally wacky gameshow-come-prank compilation. To be fair, I was taken by the one where two unlikely pugilists were openly spoofing the Takayama-Frye sequence, complete with original footage for those who didn't get the reference.

I decided I was just about with it enough to go to a wrestling show at Korakuen Hall that evening, though I nearly regretted this when I passed a steak restaurant with a sign in the window declaring a pricing policy of "6.9 yen per gram" and pretty much crashed my brain trying to figure out if this was good value.

I also passed 'British themed' pub chain Hub, which was quite the insight into how we're viewed in other cultures. As well as the supposedly-enticing opportunity to get Bass on draught, you can choose from a British food menu. Some of this is fair enough with shepherd's pie and fish and chips, albeit with a 'bite size' variant that is just goujons gone wrong. Other dishes are a little more questionable such as 'honey cheese snacks' or jacket potatoes with that well-loved traditional British topping of anchovy & mayonnaise sauce. That said, reviewing the menu now, I'm genuinely disappointed to have missed royal milk tea flavoured churros.

By now it was getting dark and the barrage of neon was making Tokyo feel that bit more, well, Tokyo-ish as I made a couple more stops on the way. First, I trawled through some backstreets looking for a FamilyMart to pick up one remaining ticket that I'd bought online, an excursion that took me past a staircase leading to the Fukumen Shop. It appeared to be a wrestling memorabilia shop, but I forgot to return later in the week to check it out. It turns out it's actually a members-only experimental-menu ramen shop where the staff all wear lucha masks. Obviously.

As for FamilyMart, I'd been reliably informed that getting the ticket simply involved using an electronic kiosk with an option to switch to English instructions. (Sadly, I didn't get any tickets from a rival chain where you have to use the menu on a photocopier.) What wasn't mentioned was that the language switch only affected the first of five levels of screens. What followed was the technological equivalent of reading a Choose Your Own Adventure book written in Japanese, though I eventually prevailed.

Last stop was a Lawson's supermarket on the bridge next to Korakuen Hall. Due no doubt both to its location and Lawson's being a New Japan sponsor, it was filled with promotional posters and banners for Wrestle Kingdom, while it appears I'd just missed the chance to see Naito's G-1 Climax briefcase on display in the entranceway. Instead I took advantage of Korakuen Hall's BYO policy and settled for grabbing a cheap and nasty sushi handroll (think Japanese equivalent of a Ginster's buffet bar). The smell of the 'seaweed' coating turned out to become a familiar aroma in the less upscale locations I visited during the week and will now be a permanent association with Tokyo in my sensory memory-bank. I also picked up a Torys Highball, which is nothing to do with the Bullingdon Club, but instead a can of whisky and soda that's seven percent and costs £1.20.

After buying my ticket at the ground floor window I returned to the fifth floor and took in Korakuen Hall with a bit more alertness than my earlier visit. As you come out of the lift you are in a small lobby (usually with desks for collecting reserved tickets) with doors to the box office and the main lobby. For this and several other shows, however, you had to take a diversion through a backroom that's packed with wrestlers selling their merchandise and promoting upcoming shows.

Once through into the main lobby, all the facilities are on one side of the main hall, with side staircases up to the two balconies and side corridors for those with ringside seats. Squeezed into the 100 feet or so between the corridors are the two stairways up to the main seating area, a food and drinks stand, a smoking room, and a display of memorabilia, most of it related to historic boxing events at the venue, despite it being primarily a wrestling venue.

Before taking my seat, I stopped off at the food stand and picked up what may be the ideal wrestling snack: a perfectly-tender pork cutlet fried in breadcrumbs, placed inside two slices of sandwich bread with a dash of barbecue sauce and then cut into bite-sized pieces. Filling, pseudo-nutritious, tidy to eat, and yours for under a fiver.

This proved to be the only show where I wasn't sat in the main ("South") seating section. The hall itself is laid out in an asymmetric manner as this South section has 18 rows of 46 seats, roughly the size and layout of a large cinema, making up around half of the venue's seating. Around the ring there's only actually three rows of chairs on the floor. On the East and West sides you then have five rows of bleacher-style wooden seating, so avoid this unless you have a particularly padded backside. (If that is the case, you may wish to give the South seating a miss as it's very much designed for Japanese-width hips.) Finally, there's a raised area on the North side that can be configured by the promotions: those expecting large crowds will use a combination of banked seating and bleachers while those with a more select appeal can curtain it off and use it as an entrance stage.

That was the case with this event from the women's WAVE promotion, which had also closed off the two standing area balconies on the East and West walls. If your knees are up to it, this appears to offer a view as good as anywhere else in the venue. And if you've ever noticed banners hung off the balcony in support of wrestlers, it turns out these are still in place even on shows when the balcony isn't open to fans. While many banners are legitimately made by the audience, this suggests it may sometimes be the promotions themselves putting them up.

After all of this it was finally time for some wrestling with WAVE's chronologically questionable Thanksgiving show (which turned out to be more about gratitude for 2017 as a whole rather than for an American harvest). I had virtually no knowledge of the promotion and thus no real expectations, but the opening eight-woman tag disproved several of my preconceptions. Based largely on my memories of AJW I was expecting plain black outfits, no discernible personalities and very basic moves. Instead I got colourfully-clad individuals with distinct characters and exciting, well-executed moves. It certainly set the tone for the rest of the week as I continued to discover that although the best British matches today are as good as anything I saw outside of Wrestle Kingdom, the lower-card Japanese performers – particularly in openers – have a level of competence at the basics that's hard to match.

The undoubted highlight of the show was a hardcore tag match with Ryo Mizunami & Rina Yamashita vs KAORU (formerly of AJW and a founder member of the Gaea promotion) & SAKI. This was a ridiculously entertaining brawl with everything from ladder dives and arena tours to one wrestler running over an opponent at ringside on a bicycle and another laying out a foe with a gigantic Chupa Chup lollipop.

The show also set me up for what would be a consistent (and welcome) pattern: every event starts at precisely the advertised time, the intervals are kept to barely 10 minutes, and it's rare that a show lasts much longer than two-and-a-half hours. I learned the hard way that it's no use waiting a few minutes during the interval to let the queues die down in the loos and at the food stands. That said I did have time to see the utter insanity of the smoking room. Tokyo's approach to smoking laws is somewhat counter to that of the UK: smoking is banned in many outdoor areas, but indoor smoking is left to the venue to police. At Korakuen Hall, the answer is a tiny internal room with no windows, jam-packed with people frantically puffing away. Although the front wall is entirely glass, it's difficult to see anyone inside through the thick fog of smoke.

The second half brought a familiar face with a guest appearance by Sendai Girls star Meiko Satomura, who – in a perfect example of the bizarrity of 2017 wrestling – I'd last seen taking on WWE titleholder Pete Dunne on a show from American promotion Chikara in a Wolverhampton nightclub.

Following the main event, it was time for a musical performance. While I was half-expecting this, it turned out not to be from the wrestlers, but rather a young lad with a guitar. It was a very mixed crowd response with the children and women on hand delighted by the appearance of what appeared to be a minor celebrity (with many holding up branded scarves). Meanwhile the men were less impressed, chief among them somebody who'd be a familiar sight among the crowds at the venue during the week, a stocky fellow who resembled a cross between Tomohiro Ishii and Kim Jong-Un. He had a permanently grumpy expression, but all the more so as he watched the concert with defiantly crossed arms. After the second song concluded and the performance showed no signs of ending, I took his point and made a polite exit to head for my bed. It turned out this was a smart decision as the evening concluded with a ceremony to run down the top ten rankings for the year, something that would no doubt have turned my micro-dozes during the later matches into a full-blown snoreathon.

Saturday 30th December

My phone keeps a text and audio record of every enquiry you make to its virtual assistant. I know this as my history for this day begins with the words "OK Google, is it ok to wear pajamas in japanese hotel lobby." Sadly, the answer is no.

Said visit was to take advantage of the free breakfast bar that excitingly promised "six types of bread." This turned out to be one type of bread (the Japanese equivalent of Warburton's blandest white sandwich bread) and five flavours of pastry, namely "plain", "chocolate", "very artificial strawberry", "not quite right lemon" and "oh god, I've not tasted curry like that since school."

Welcome as free carbs always are, there was something of a prison feel in the small room. The only seating was fixed stools beneath benches around the wall, with nobody making eye contact, instead staring at a TV set mounted by the ceiling. Meanwhile the only non-'bread' foods were hard boiled eggs and grated cheese, which slightly baffled me until I saw Japanese guests topping bread with ketchup, sprinkling cheese on top, putting it in a toaster oven and making the type of monstrosity you could convince yourself was 'pizza' when you still had the bulk of an eight stretch to serve.

As for Japan's breakfast TV, it was closer to This Morning's magazine format than Good Morning Britain, with the unlikely highlight being a visit to a department store to learn the geometric secrets of efficiently fitting the maximum number of Tupperware display items on a single table. With, as you've no doubt guessed, a backing track of Stop by the Spice Girls.

Having woken early and having a couple of hours until the first show at noon, I went for a walk to tick off a few of the places on my to-do list. First was the bookshop district of Jimbocho where I was looking for what was billed as the biggest bookshop in town. As I approached it from an alleyway, I found a covered display of magazines including several piles of early 1980s Weekly Pro and Gong wrestling magazines for the equivalent of a couple of pounds. Frustratingly I turned the corner to find that I wasn't by the bookshop at all. Instead the covered display was a standalone stall that was shut for the day – and which I failed to find again later in the week.

I did have more luck visiting Budokan Hall, which is just inside the grounds of what was Edo Castle, which used to be the country's military headquarters when Tokyo was known as Edo. While the castle itself is long gone, a few parts of the boundary structure remain in place, and to get to Budokan itself you need to walk over a moat and then through two enormous 17th century gates. To say the least, it's a bit different from going through Penn Station to get to Madison Square Garden.

My first visit to Korakuen Hall was for DDT DAMNATION Produce Illegal Gathering Vol 2, which turned out to be a special NWO Souled Out-like show where the DAMNATION faction – having won a previous contest – got to book the event. Things didn't really go to plan for them though: Daisuke Sasaki lost his Extreme (aka hardcore) title in the main event, while Mad Paulie (who resembled a knock-off Bam Bam Bigelow figure) recruited two guest 'Mad Paulies' (one of them the 32-stone Ryota Hama) but failed to win the six-man titles. Shuji Ishikawa had a bit more luck, bringing in All Japan's Suwama to destroy the Brahman Brothers, two fellows whose main schtick is drenching the crowd with buckets of water as well as using a baseball bat to smash oranges into pulp that flies into the stands.

As you'd expect, the show also had some outright comedy including a costume battle royale, though it was largely lost on me as I knew none of the participants and few of the people they dressed as, though regular DDT viewers assured me it was a real hoot. Meanwhile a tag match with Dick Togo and Colt Cabana included a four-way Dusty elbow sequence and a brief intermission while Antonio Honda did a series of impressions of Star Wars characters for no discernible reason.

After stopping for a quick chat with Colt Cabana in the lobby, I took the stairs rather than the lift. All four floors of the stairway are absolutely covered in graffiti by wrestling fans and I even spotted a picture making the somewhat questionable claim that Britain's Jason Cross was the number one gaijin wrestler of 1998. I later discovered this had been written by my friend Phil Jones and on another climb, I spotted the signatures that he and Ollie Hurley had made on a trip at the turn of the century.

I then got down to the serious business of exploring the streets just across the river from Tokyo Dome City, which house several wrestling-related venues, including Toru Yano's bar EBRIETAS; it was closed so I shrugged my shoulders, raised my palms to the air, raised my eyebrows and left. My first stop was instead the official New Japan store, complete with a sign making it very clear the New Year's Dash show was long since sold out. Stairway graffiti was on display again, though this time it appeared to all be by wrestlers, with Drake Younger, 2 Tuff Tony, Mad Man Mondo and Tessa Blanchard having all paid a visit.

The shop itself was a little disappointing as it was absolutely tiny and was mainly filled with current t-shirts and hoodies, with a range no bigger than you'd expect to see at the merch table at a show, though you could also pick up the branded IWGP cologne "King of King". One highlight was mini-museum area including an original IWGP title belt, a North American tag title belt held by Antonio Inoki and Seiji Sakaguchi, and a poster for the Inoki-Ali match that had been signed by both men.

Immediately round the corner from the New Japan shop was a wrestling video and DVD store where I got to see the original packaging for many of the mid-90s titles that I viewed through not-entirely-legitimate means. Buying a DVD was out of the question given the ludicrous prices, while the video tapes seemed much more affordable until I discovered they were rental-only.

These disappointments were long forgotten when I visited the Toudoukan ('Champions') shop, which is absolutely packed with virtually every wrestling item you can imagine, past and present. To try to give some sort of scale, there are entire aisles dedicated to t-shirts, autographs, masks, action figures, programs, books, video tapes, DVDs & CDs, and magazines. Between the shelves and the stockroom, the shop has more than 50,000 items.

It also has several display cases around the edge of the room that contain items that are technically for sale but are so highly-priced they serve as exhibits. They included Great Muta headgear, numerous ring-worn Tiger Masks, the boots worn by Carlos Colon in his final match, Rikidozan's Japanese passport, Hisashi Shinma's business card as WWWF president, and even a plate from Antonio Inoki's wedding reception, yours for a mere £516.

While I'd sworn off acquiring "stuff" having just moved house on only a couple of weeks' notice (which included three divorce-threatening car journeys just to move my wrestling magazines and newsletters) I did allow myself one purchase and began hunting for a program. One from the very first New Japan show in 1972 was available but sadly out of my price range, so I instead decided it was appropriate to get one from the first Tokyo Dome show in 1989. Even here I had a choice of three options, depending on what inserts I wanted, opting for one with a copy of the original match running order sheet that set me back just over £10.

Meanwhile the lobby outside the store was covered in hand-made posters advertising what I suspect may have been less-than-stellar wrestling organizations. One was the "Dr Keita in The House School of Wrestling", complete with early 1990s WWF logo. Dr Keita had also got himself a main event booking as part of the Lucha Wannabee Order, taking on The Crippler and X-Law in an "Eddie Guerrero Tribute Match" at LWO Homecoming, held in a small dance studio. Intrigued as I was, the show had taken place the previous week.

I tore myself away in time to go hunting for food around Korakuen Hall where I discovered that while much of the surrounding area is made up of ultra-clean chain restaurants and food courts serving the Tokyo Dome, immediately under the bridge that leads to the venues is a grimy bookmaker's. If it's hundreds of slightly tipsy chain-smokers eating questionable meats while clawing on to a betting slip you want, be sure to check it out.

I played it safe and went to the food court, though admittedly that was mainly because I couldn't resist seeing what was served in a restaurant named "Bikkuri Donkey Pocket." I wound up with the unlikely pairing of a hamburger in curry sauce and jolly tasty it was too.

Heading into the show I was again diverted through the merchandise room, which was also filled with wrestlers from the Ice Ribbon promotion doing an incredible job of shilling tickets for the following day's event.

I'd got my ticket for the evening from Japanican, a tourist service that books activities such as trips to Mount Fuji or watching sumo and was offering a discount on the wrestling. As well as the ticket, they'd provided a handy seating plan of the hall (complete with the Japanese symbols used for row and section details) and a sheet explaining how long the show would last and warning me not to go into the ring or to hassle wrestlers for autographs. All of this would have been perfectly normal were it not for the fact that unsuspecting tourists booking for the show were pitched on it being a traditional cultural experience. Goodness only knows what they think when they then see Big Japan Pro-Wrestling.

(I got tickets for a Big Japan show later in the week by buying direct from their website, paying online and collecting on the night, which all ran smoothly. The only real downside was explaining why my next credit card statement had an entry for 'BJ Shop'.)

Big Japan is known for its split between the death match and strong style divisions, but it was the latter which made up the undercard, the most impressive appearance being a fellow in a 'Catch As Catch Can' hoodie named Hideki Suzuki. Little was I to realise just how familiar I would become with him over the week. The violence was instead saved for a truly spectacular main event, a 12-man Year End Death Rumble which was the same as the Royal Rumble but with every competitor bringing their own weapons.

These included one wrestler using a fishing rod to literally fishhook an opponent from across the ring, while another scattered what looked like pine cones across the ring, the only thing that made wrestlers flee. It turns out said items are used for flower arranging and have dozens of incredibly sharp points. Then the 75-year-old Great Kojika turned up, got annoyed by the younger, kinder wrestlers refusing to attack him, and poured a bag of drawing pins over his own head. The drama ended with Abdullah Kobayashi opening up a crate of fluorescent light tubes, with which he finished off all remaining opponents for the win. While I was reminded of Dave Bond's polite assessment of Big Daddy that "he wasn't really a technician", it was undoubtedly enjoyable as a spectacle.

With the show finishing around 9pm, I decided it was time to be spontaneous and explore further afield in Tokyo. This did not prove an overwhelming success.

My first move was to a small bar in a non-descript neighbourhood, which I visited for perfectly ludicrous reasons. By going to Tokyo, I'd had to withdraw from a bi-annual New Year holiday with my wife's friends from university, which is usually preceded by a two-year long challenge. This time it was to take a photograph of yourself having a drink in a particular named pub. My wife had been assigned The King's Arms and had not quite taken the challenge as seriously as some of her friends. Discovering that a tiny English-style pub of that name could be found in an obscure backstreet, I decided to at least earn her credit by osmosis.

"Could be found" proved an understatement as the journey first involved consulting Google Maps and freaking out to see several swastika logos in the local area before eventually realising they merely indicated Hindu temples. I then had to make my way over a pelican crossing that covered eight lanes of traffic in one go, a task made harder by the realisation that in Tokyo red and green lights are not so much orders about how drivers should behave, but instead no more than a suggestion as to who would be held legally responsible were a vehicle and pedestrian to collide.

Eventually I found the pub, which was shut for New Year. Disheartened I returned to the subway and consoled myself with a Cornetto-style chocolate ice cream from a vending machine. In hindsight, buying an ice cream on the day before New Year's Eve makes little sense, but I was responding to a double dose of novelty. Firstly, it was the only time during the trip that I saw a vending machine selling anything other than drinks, despite all the talk of machines carrying everything from popcorn to used knickers. Secondly, the machine accepted payment from my contactless travel card, which of course doesn't really count as spending.

The ice cream was naturally rock solid despite my warming it with both hands, until of course the moment it suddenly wasn't and my hands were completely coated. With no bathroom or wet wipes available, I was left cleaning them up by tongue. As the journey continued, I got a few funny looks until I saw my reflection and realised I had inadvertently recreated a certain sitcom scene. Naturally I took full advantage of the language barrier, smiled at my fellow passengers, and said "It may be chocolate to you Jill, but to an unwitting member of staff this could look like some sort of dirty protest..."

The subway runs as smoothly as Tokyo stereotypes would suggest, with one impressive element being a waist-high barrier along the edge of the platform that stop anyone getting on the track. It has gates that open when the train has arrived, lining up perfectly with the doors every time. Incidentally, while it's true that many trains have women-only carriages, these tend to only be operational on specific journeys in specific circumstances (generally during the rush hour morning commute) and usually won't be a problem (or a help depending on your perspective) after around 9.30 am.

Another highlight was an advertising poster on the train carriage wall in which one suited business man was unmistakably holding another in a Boston Crab. I later learned that by coincidence it was promoting an English language school where WWF wrestler Chyna once worked.

I was heading for Shibuya Crossing, star of many films and the closest thing to the definitive Tokyo landmark. It was just as I arrived at Shinjuku station that I thought twice about where it was actually located, so switched lines and went instead to Shibuya. Here I emerged from the station and walked round in a large circle, encountering a building site and several areas underneath rail tracks, but nothing resembling a landmark. With the last trains imminent, I abandoned the search and returned to Korakuen having spent more than two hours seeing little and achieving less. I then found that the welcoming bar besides Korakuen Hall that I had my eye on had now closed at 11, as had the adjacent convenience store. What I didn't know was that the 7-11 by my hotel opened into the early hours, raising questions about its name. Then again, I had come across one bar whose opening times were listed as "14:00 to 26:00".

By this point I was done with spontaneity as a concept and headed for bed.

Sunday 31st December

I woke up late and left my hotel room at 11.42 am for a noon show. In many places this would spell disaster but between my having found the quickest route through Tokyo Dome City and Japanese culture being ridiculously efficient, I was able to get to the venue, pick up a traditional breakfast of chilled coffee and chicken nuggets, collect my ticket and take my seat, all inside 12 minutes.

As with several smaller promotions, all-women's group Ice Ribbon was putting on its biggest show of the year to take advantage of the New Year wrestling season, calling it simply RibbonMania. A banner proclaimed the company slogan as "Be Happy With Pro Wrestling" and I was down with that, enjoying the show immensely despite (or perhaps because of) having limited expectations. As with every show at Korakuen Hall during the week, fans threw streamers before every bout and I noticed for the first time that they are nearly all coordinated with the colours worn by the wrestlers in question. I then amused myself with the thought of the rookies who retrieve the streamers from the ring painstakingly rolling each one back into a coil to be sold again at the next show, and frankly if that's not what happens, I don't want to know.

Among the more notable elements of the show was – I am reliably informed – an appearance by a wrestler who was just 14. That meant the oldest and youngest wrestlers I've ever seen came on consecutive shows. That also means I've seen a wrestler who was born not only after WCW's demise, but after John Cena and Randy Orton started on WWE television.

The unlikely highlight given the nature of the promotion was that man Hideki Suzuki again. He had been challenged by Ice Ribbon mainstay Miyako Matsumoto for – as best I could tell from the pre-match video – no better reason than that the pair debuted within a few months of each other. With his 140-pounds and 13-inch advantage, Suzuki won in with a legsweep in just six seconds, prompting Matsumoto to beg for a rematch, which had the same result but a second quicker. A third and final bout again saw the legsweep but Matsumoto escaped just before the count of three and the pair then put together an entertaining David vs Goliath match, highlighted by a grounded Matsumoto recreating the Ali-Inoki 'crab kicks', with the crowd fully on board with the homage.

Following the show, the crew not only gathered to shake hands with ringsiders, but even made their way up the aisles to personally thank everyone in attendance. Meanwhile, checking Twitter gave me a quick reminder of how time is a relative construct: I'd seen a full show in Tokyo that day before the previous night's UFC in Las Vegas had finished. (I also discovered that Twitter's location-based advertising has the fundamental flaw that it can't tell the difference between being in Japan and speaking Japanese.)

The evening's show at Korakuen was a late start, so I had time to take the subway and squeeze in another show at Ichigaya. One the way over I saw one of only two homeless people I spotted during my trip, with this one standing out as being remarkably neat and organized. I also only saw two people with obvious physical disabilities during the trip; on further investigation when I returned home, I learned this was likely no coincidence, with something of a stigma about disability. Indeed, just two years ago a man broke into a home for disabled people and killed 19 people in their sleep; it was Japan's biggest mass-murder since the second world war, but it received shockingly little public attention.

Ichigaya is certainly not a favourite tourist district, housing a couple of universities and the country's Ministry of Defense. Even in this nondescript area, I was heading for a more obscure location, following instructions to head up an alleyway between a convenience store and a burger chain outlet. Looking round the unmarked buildings I was greeted by a shy-looking woman and a man who uttered the word I wanted to hear, "Puroresu?"

I recognised the woman as Gatoh Move promoter Emi Sakura and the three of us began a particularly awkward conversation. The problem was that I perfectly understood (or rather deduced) what was being said in Japanese, namely that I was too early and would have to return in 20 minutes. Unfortunately, I didn't know how to convey that I understood the message and that nobody needed to feel any embarrassment. Instead I wasted time pondering whether it was worth taking advantage of the fact that I did know how to cobble together the sentence "I don't not understand." If you're wondering how successfully this went, let's just say that before the day was done, Pro Wrestling EVE's Dann Read had been informed by Sakura via Facebook Messenger that he had a blundering compatriot.

Once I returned at the correct time, I was ready for the somewhat complicated entry procedure of collecting my pre-booked ticket; handing my shoulder bag into the makeshift cloakroom (the fact that somebody as neurotic as me was comfortable letting their passport and a sizeable amount of cash out of my sight tells you how safe Tokyo feels); and waiting for my entry number to be called. This was a satisfying process in that it justified my having learned Japanese numbers up to 99, while a couple of Americans on hand missed their spot.

The order of entry was important as the venue, despite the curious name of the Ichigaya Chocolate Plaza, was in fact a makeshift room in a former pharmacy. And we're talking the type of tiny pharmacy you'd see next to a GP's surgery rather than a branch of Boots. It was about as big as what you'd describe as a decent sized living room, something like 20 feet by twelve feet, with two solid walls and then plate glass with a door at the front where the 'shop window' used to be (and through which both the crowd and wrestlers entered.)

Normally Japanese wrestling attendances are announced with misleading terms such as "No Vacancy" referring to at least 90 percent capacity (with a true sellout being "Super No Vacancy".) When running Tokyo, Gatoh Move prefers "crowded", "over crowded" and "super crowded." This show's attendance of 73 fell in to the latter category. Three sides of the room had a single row of stools, with everyone else standing behind them squeezed against the wall. If you've been keeping count and wondering what happened with the wall on the other side of the room, it originally had two windows. These have now been removed allowing fans to stand outside in the street and lean in to watch the action.

As is often the case with women's promotions, the show began with the very small core roster putting on a song and dance performance, a fair description of which would be "enthusiastic". The crew then passed out handwarmers before the first match, which turned out to be an all-male affair.

Oh right, you're wondering how they got the ring in, aren't you?

There was no ring. Instead the matches (and everything else) took place on a crash mat on the floor that was maybe 12 feet by six feet. It turns out you don't actually need a ring to put on a match, not even when the ceiling is too low for a vertical suplex. The actual mechanics of telling a story, building up comebacks and cheating behind a referee's back all work in even the most confined space.

Indeed, the second match – also man vs man – got even more creative. The fans in the front row acted as a ring rope, pushing back wrestlers who were 'springing off the ropes'. Meanwhile the window ledges served as a top rope for some limited aerial moves. And the creativity peaked when the pair brawled out the front door and round the side of the building before one grappler performed a jumping Canadian Destroyer through the window frame and on to the 'ring mat'.

That said, this was one of the more conventional shows Gatoh Move has run in the venue. Normally the second match on the three-bout cards will have a bizarre gimmick such as pinfalls not ending the match but rather earning a wrestler the right to attempt a game of charades to get the victory.

Despite the constrained space, the main event here was a six-person tag consisting of the five regulars on the roster and DDT male grappler Toru Owashi, who's every bit of his billed 6'1" and 242 pounds. Somehow, they made it work despite the size difference, with the highlight being several pairs of wrestlers doing the traditional AJW rolling cradle spot, only to crash straight into the wall.

Once the matches were over, it was time for everyone in the room to get a cup of tea before another song and dance number. The wrestlers then all received personalised presents from the promotion to celebrate the end of the year and then it was raffle time. Well, not quite. Shocking as it was for a British fan to not see a single raffle all week, I had to settle for a room-wide elimination series of rock-paper-scissors with the winner getting a signed drawing of the crew. Unfortunately, this was one time when the language barrier proved fatal. I couldn't quite work out if the idea was that you had to beat the 'leader' to stay on to the next round, or merely avoid losing to their choice, so when I matched their selection I tactically withdrew rather than risk an international incident. The three-match show lasted for barely an hour, but I doubt you'll see anything quite like Gatoh Move anywhere else.

I returned to the hotel to warm up, bumping into a fellow Brit named Mark – or as I knew him, 'Monkeybuckles' from Twitter – and having a quick chat where I tried to convey some of the insanity I'd just seen. (By a weird coincidence I turned out to be sat next to Mark and another Brit named Stuart that evening.)

I then went back to Korakuen Hall via the food court where this time I opted for beef curry. Of course, there was a twist: this was curry made from beef tendons, a dish that may be structurally repellent but makes up for it in taste. I also spotted a bar whose menu had a 'HARD TYPE' section with an 'Alcoholicity Ranking Best 5', appropriately topped by a drink named 'Dynamite Kid'.

New Year's Eve at Korakuen Hall is now a longstanding tradition in which independent promotions led by DDT put on a show with an unusual set-up. Previous years had seen a 108-man rumble (the number being considered lucky in Japanese New Year tradition), a show-long Domino Rally storyline, and a five-a-side football match. This year's offering was the snappily-titled 'Toshikoshi Pro Wrestling 2017 – Toshiwasure! Two Organization Shuffle Tag Tournament.'

This was a 16-team elimination tournament with each 'randomly selected' pairing involving one wrestler from DDT and one from Big Japan. This produced some unlikely pairing such as the aggressively homosexual Danshoku Dino and the (as it were) straight-laced Daichi Hashimoto, son of Shinya, as well as the comedic Colt Cabana teaming with ultra-violent Abdullah Kobayashi.

With plenty of matches to get through, it was something of a sprint with every bout either being a quality hard-hitting, technical grappling affair, or people just pissing about, such as the Brahman Brothers upping the ante by pelting opponents and fans alike with what appeared to be rancid fish. The most heated first round affair involved Hideki Suzuki and Konosuke Takeshita going to a 10-minute draw with the Great Kojika and Tetsuya Endo, which prompted an overtime period where a one-count would win it; Kojika got the fall but the referee missed it and he was soon eliminated.

The highlight of the quarter-final round, and indeed of the night, involved Kobayashi and Cabana coming to the ring in cosplay mode, the twist being that Cabana dressed as Abdullah the Butcher (Kobayashi's usual influence) while Kobayashi performed as Stan Hansen. Appropriately Hideki and Takeshita then emerged as Bruiser Brody and Jimmy Snuka respectively, with the four men engaging in an arena brawl so true to early '80s All Japan that it even ended in a double disqualification. The dig at booking of the era continued when the match was restarted to make sure somebody advanced, with 'Snuka' barely making it back in the ring in time for a countout win.

To give a break between the quarter-finals and semi-finals, the presenters of Occupation Of The Indiez (a cable TV news show dedicated to smaller wrestling promotions) came to the ring to present the show's year-end awards. Those presenters being one woman and one puppet of a purple mole-like creature. Things got even more surreal when the best newcomer award was won by Andre The Giant Panda, who had several matches despite being a man in a 10-foot-tall panda costume. Sadly, he was unable to accept the award in person.

Meanwhile the breathing room between semi-final and final came with an eight-man tag match to celebrate Taka Michinoku's 25th anniversary as a wrestler. Predictably this ended in comedy with one competitor trapped in the corner and then hit with running strikes first by all of his opponents, then by as many other wrestlers on the show as could make it down to ringside before it was time to hit a roll-up for the finish, with the three count suspiciously coming on the exact stroke of midnight.

Four hours in to the show it was time for the final, with Suzuki (in technically his seventh match of the day) and Takeshita taking the win, meaning that I could not only say I'd been there live for the undisputed match of the year, but for a brief few hours I'd seen every match that had taken place in the world during 2018.

Monday 1st January 2018

That record might have continued had I stuck to my original plan for another triple-shot day, but in the end, I settled for just the one show. The day could have started with a small independent promotion named YMZ that was running a show at the curious time of 7.50am, something I didn't really understand until I saw the show was described as a sunrise festival. As it was taking place seven miles from my hotel at Shin-Kiba 1st Ring, I would have needed to leave around 6.30 to be sure of making the start, and when the idea came to reality, that simply wasn't happening.

I also had a reservation for a noon show but gave it a miss for several reasons. One was that even though it would have been a short event, it would have been a very tight journey to get back to Korakuen Hall where I had a 2pm show. Another was that the venue was simply listed as "the basement of the subway at Shinjuku station" and my attempts to get clarification fell on deaf ears. As we'll see later, those directions would have been about as helpful as being told a show was somewhere in the Twilight Zone.

But I will admit the final straw was the nature of the show. I booked thinking it was 666, one of the smaller offshoots of DDT that would earn me a few hipster points for obscurity. In fact, it turned out to be 2-Cho Pro Wrestling, an offshoot of 666. The name refers to 2-Chome, Tokyo's main gay district (a little like if Futureshock in Manchester launched Canal Street Pro Wrestling), and the events are sponsored by a leading gay lifestyle magazine.

Now, I certainly have no moral objection to such a show and I was still considering going until I read a report of a previous show in which matches included a sadists vs masochists battle, the 'Large Penis Collectors Team' taking on the 'Fully Erect Under The Pants Team', and the main event battle royale with elimination by pinfall, submission or having your trunks removed. Seeing such an affair would be one thing. Paying £35 for the privilege would be quite another.

For the sake of posterity, it's worth noting a few other shows I didn't make on the trip. On the first morning I'd planned to go to Hard Hit, a UWF-i like shoot-style promotion. Unfortunately, I'd missed the deadline for buying tickets and as it was in a small venue I didn't want to risk it being sold out on the door. It turns out that had I gone, I would have started my Hideki Suzuki marathon a few hours earlier.

I also rejected one women's wrestling show when I saw the cover of their most recent DVD release; Brits who remember the extremely expensive shows put on by Pippa L'Vinn will catch my drift. I also spotted a show by the DIANA promotion, which has several familiar names from the glory days of AJW. I was somewhat thrown by the show description informing fans to "bring a towel and change of shoes" and it wasn't until I saw the request "also, please be a woman" that I clocked this was in fact a training seminar.

With the morning free, I took the opportunity to have a much-needed bath. There was no bathtap as such, with the tub instead filled from the showerhead. Let's just say that it fills much quicker than you'd expect, that the power of a jet of running water can tilt a showerhead, and that I now have the dubious honour of having flooded bathrooms on three continents.

The day's only show was from Zero One, which has fallen somewhat from its peak period, only achieving a half-full crowd at Korakuen (whereas the previous night's show was almost sold out). It was still perfectly enjoyable, with pre-show and interval entertainment coming from an all-female band who spiced up their own repertoire by throwing in Riki Choshu's ring music and Sky High, the legendary music used by Mil Mascaras (and surely the greatest Bond movie theme that never was.)

The show itself had a bit of everything. I saw Shinjiro Otani for the first time since 2000 when a friend booked him against Christopher Daniels at the Skydome largely for his own entertainment. Hideki Suzuki popped up, as you'd expect. A wrestler named SUGI did the best huracanrana (straight into a pin) that I've seen since Rey Mysterio Jr and Psicosis debuted in the ECW Arena. And Masato Tanaka put on a great main event appearance despite the fact he's 45 and by all rights should have neither his mental nor physical faculties at this point.

I also had the opportunity to pick up a few more insights into the Japanese wrestling culture. For example, as well as the timekeeper ringing the bell five times to mark the official start of the show, on this occasion at least it appeared that the more times he rung it to mark the end of a match, the better he thought the bout had been. The crowd continued the pattern of an increasing minority of Western fans during the week and it struck home for the first time that I'd seen fewer than five children across the shows. Whenever a wrestler blew a spot, the crowd's reaction was an "ooh" of disappointment rather than mocking or anger. Unlike New Japan's patterns, this show had the first teased countout spot of the week. And when two wrestlers brawled into the crowd and began seizing chairs to throw at one another, venue staff retrieved them from the ring and replaced them all in to their original perfectly aligned rows within mere moments.

The show also served as a landmark as it meant I had finally achieved seven live shows in seven days. In fact, it was seven shows in seventy-one hours. And I was only half-way through the schedule.

Even though it was one of the longer shows of the trip, the 5.30 finish was the earliest I would end my wrestling 'commitments' during the week, so I took the chance to explore the city further, starting with Shibuya where I finally found the correct exit for the famous crossing. Part of my confusion came when, after puzzling as to why the main East and West exits were clearly mislabelled, I realised that the maps around the station had South at the top, something I quite literally couldn't get my head around for some time.

The crossing itself is worth a visit, though perhaps not quite as insane as I'd been led to believe (once you get past the young men racing around in miniature Mario Karts that is.) It's simply a large intersection of several major roads with five pelican crossings where, rather than cycle round each road in turn, all the crossings activate at the same time with traffic coming to a standstill and hundreds of pedestrians (at peak time more than a thousand) crossing at once. Viewed from above it's a compelling pattern, a little like a murmuration of birds.

In theory you should be getting collisions everywhere, but the secret is that Japanese people appear to trust in the maths that if everyone walks at their own pace, picking a straight line at a slightly different angle to the person next to them and sticking to it, there's mathematically very little chance of two people being in the same spot at the same time. The problem comes with Westerners who panic and try to change course to avoid collisions. Lesson for Japan: don't worry about the "step left or step right when someone's coming towards you" dilemma and instead just keep heading straight on. Albeit with your fingers crossed.

I then looked around the shops (much of Shibuya is reminiscent of London's Oxford Street) including a Tower Records. Back in the day it was a treat to go to the one in Piccadilly and a mindblowing experience to visit the giant branches in New York. Today the entire concept of physical media feels bizarrely outdated in a supposedly futuristic city. I did toy with the novelty of rebuying Deep Purple's Made In Japan in, well, Japan, but it wasn't a novelty worth £20.

Several of the places I'd earmarked for dinner were shut for the day, most notably one which was themed on the 47 prefectures of Japan, with a tapas-style selection of authentic local dishes from each. By now I was getting desperate for the loo, leading to a truly baffling 20 minutes as I went into Shibuya station and followed the signs for the toilets. I'd been twice round the station (the world's fourth largest) before I realised I was going in a loop and it took another circuit before I finally realised that all the toilet facilities were for 'proven' passengers only and thus were the wrong side of the ticket barriers.

Not quite ready to leave yet, I instead found facilities at the top of a multi-storey book and CD store that produced another surprise. In this age of streaming music subscription services, some people in Tokyo still rent physical CDs.

Yes, that's right, rent.

Bladder and curiosity satisfied, I took a train over to Shinjuku where the first challenge was exiting the station. If Shibuya is the developmental territory for rail passengers, Shinjuku is the WrestleMania of commuting. It's the world's biggest and busiest station complex by some margin and when it comes to the figures, nobody can quite seem to agree. It connects directly to between five and 10 other railway and subway stations (depending on who's counting), meaning you can change between more than 50 platforms without going out into the street. When you are ready to leave, you have more than 200 exits to choose from, many of which go through department stores.

To add to the fun, some exits are off walkways above the train platforms while others are below. There's only a few places where you can switch between the two sets of walkways, meaning that if you don't grasp the layout or you've missed a switching point, you could literally walk for miles in a forlorn hunt for a particular exit. Fortunately, I won this particular challenge and found my intended destination of Omoide Yokocho where I could satisfy my growing hunger to get some cheap and dirty food inside me.

Omoide Yokocho, which translates as Memory Lane, is simultaneously the most authentic and artificial destination in Tokyo's culinary world. It dates back to the 1940s when it was a side street approaching the station, filled with low-cost bars of questionable licensing status and extremely basic food joints – effectively a Japanese take on the rows of kebab shops and not-even-Wetherspoons pubs that you'll find approaching stations in run down British seaside towns. It was (and apparently still is) better known as Piss Alley by locals, a throwback to the era when the bars didn't have room for toilets so customers would relieve themselves in the street, behind the bars, or even onto the passing train tracks.

Despite the surrounding area becoming an extremely gentrified land of towering chrome and neon, the alleyway remained unchanged until a 1999 fire, after which the local government rebuilt it on the same spot as an exact replica. It's effectively a tiny time capsule that's just yards from 21st century streets and could almost feel like visiting a tourist attraction were it not for the fact that it's still a working area.

The rebuilt Omoide Yokocho now has two extremely narrow alleys absolutely packed with dozens of tiny bars and restaurants either side. Perhaps fortunately I didn't come across Asadachi, which translates as Morning Wood and specialises in dishes such as frog sashimi, pig testicles and horse penis. While to Westerners it's something of a Bush Tucker Trial experience, its origins are as a way for commuting 'salarymen' to give themselves some extra sexual energy before completing their journey home and performing their marital duties.

Instead I went to a restaurant that I couldn't name and probably couldn't find again. It was no more than five feet across, with diners sat along a bench running the length of the room and their backs almost touching the wall, meaning everyone had to squeeze forwards if anyone wanted to enter or leave. The middle of the bench had a short glass partition, immediately behind which was a grill, with the chef stood behind (around 18 inches from my face) and equally close to the opposing wall.

Although I was given a menu to leaf through with dozens of dishes, this appeared to be purely ceremonial as any non-Japanese customers were informed they would be having the set menu. This consisted of a token starter of some sort of pickled vegetable (a mandatory purchase for all guests that acted as a cover charge) followed by a yakitori selection – in other words meat on sticks. This included chicken wings, minced chicken balls, pork belly, pork... something, and leeks, all of which were waved in the general direction of flames just long enough to get a tan before being dipped in a sticky sauce of unknown provenance. Including a beer, the whole thing cost me less than £14. I wouldn't suspect environmental health inspectors would be too impressed with the entire setup, and a Japanese man hocking up a spectacular loogie on the floor as I left was a little too authentic for my taste, but sometimes you just want food that's absolutely filthy in a good way.

Time was now pressing for the final trains, so I just had long enough to walk a mile or so to find a bar that a friend who lived in Tokyo for several months had recommended – indeed insisted – that I visit. It was closed for the New Year holiday, but I did see enough of the area to get the distinct impression the regulars would have enjoyed the 2-Cho show more than I would have.

Instead I stopped off at the convenience store by Korakuen Hall where I bumped into Zack Sabre Jr. (Fortunately I was now off the Tory Highball drinks, instead going for cans of triple-strength Kirin beer that had grapefruit juice added to make it palatable.) It was the first time we'd met, so what did I talk about with one of the finest technical grapplers in the world today? Yep, the psychology of using light tubes as weapons.

Tuesday 2nd January

The bad news was that I discovered the random nature of jetlag, only getting two hours' sleep. The good news that even in near-zombie mode, I was now fully adjusted to my new normality and could simply head to Korakuen Hall at noon without even having to think about it.

The first show of the day was All Japan and the first thing to take in was just how different the crowd was to that for other promotions. It was the first show to have a significant number of families with young children on hand. It was the first to have large numbers of men drinking at lunchtime. And it was the first to have a queue for the ladies' toilets at the interval.

Given the crowd mix, plus the fact many of the Japanese spectators were being shown to their seat (a job I could probably qualify for now), I got the impression this was a particularly 'casual' audience, most likely families attending as a New Year treat similar to Brits going to the panto, with All Japan being the promotion parents remembered from their youth. Indeed, it was the only show where wrestlers received boos and catcalls. And it even had the ring announcer opening things up with the traditional British family show "Which side of the crowd can cheer loudest?" schtick.

(This was also the first show where you could hear American fans shouting supposedly-witty comments. Fortunately, it was only a couple of occasions and got a silent reaction, which shouldn't have been a surprise given they were shouting in English…)

It's certainly not 1994 anymore, but there was still enough tradition and nostalgia for me to enjoy the All Japan experience. The first match was something of a legends checklist with Osamu Nishimura, Ultimo Dragon (who I last saw in Saltford Village Hall), Dick Togo and Masanobu Fuchi. Seeing Fuchi was a sobering sight as I recalled that back in the Hulk Who? fanzine days we'd mockingly refer to him as Masanobu Forty because he looked so old. I can't say I ever imagined I'd see him wrestle live when I was in my 40s.

I also got to see the annual battle royale, which has a reputation for being awful thanks to the rule that you can be eliminated via pinfall, which inevitably leads to mass pile-ons for every cover. On this occasion they made the most of it, with the psychology being that wrestlers were trying to engineer a rival to be the victim of a mob attack without attracting enough attention to become the target themselves.

The match also had a fun sequence with wrestlers lining up to be bodyslammed by Fuchi in the manner of the Four Horsemen all taking a Dusty elbow. All went well until either the musclebound Bodyguard or the 331-pound Yutaka Yoshie got to the front of the line.

The main event was a chance to tick 'Triple Crown Defence' off the bucket list with Joe Doering facing the challenge of 'Not That One' Zeus. This was one of the better matches of the week despite – or perhaps because of – the first 16 minutes or so of the 20-minute match consisting solely of chops, clotheslines and the occasional suplex. The physicality built and the near falls at the end garnered by far the loudest reaction of any of the Korakuen Hall events I attended. The entire show went barely over two hours but didn't feel too short or insubstantial whatsoever.

I was feeling too tired to go too far afield in the afternoon, so I stuck to walking around the nearby neighbourhoods of Suidobashi and Jimbocho. One highlight was Shosen Grande (the shop I'd been searching for on the first morning), whose multiple floors include a basement with a wrestling section that has a vast selection of photo magazines along with several dozen autobiographies of Japanese wrestlers. (A newsagent right by Korakuen Hall also had a wrestling book table right as you walked in, though I wasn't sure if this was because of the location or because it was Wrestle Kingdom week.)

Unfortunately for an English speaker there is a fairly fundamental flaw with Japanese books, particularly those that are almost entirely text, so I had to give them a miss. The good news is that one of the most intriguing was the autobiography of New Japan booker Gedo. Since I returned, Chris Charlton – a Westerner living in Tokyo – has been posting translated highlights on his Twitter account at @reasonjp.

I also visited a 100-yen store where I'd hoped to find some utterly tacky tat to bring back as presents. Annoyingly the chain I visited, Can*Do, turned out be full of genuinely useful stuff, a bit like visiting a branch of The Range or Wilkinsons where everything cost 70 pence. Stifling rents aside, there are definitely plenty of aspects of daily life where Tokyo could be surprisingly affordable. (I did calculate that I'd only have to earn £500 a month more to be able to afford a studio apartment within walking distance of Korakuen Hall and then attend every show. Unfortunately, neither Japanese immigration law nor my wife are down with this.)

There was also just enough time for a second look round Toudoukan, which was inevitably becoming a popular destination with the increasing number of Western arrivals. For the most part, they were all friendly enough, and while emerging from the lift into my hotel lobby in the morning to be greeted by a passionate discussion about the merits of the belt worn by the Western States Heritage champion wasn't my cup of tea (at that time of day, a cup of tea was more my cup of tea), it wasn't doing anyone any harm. However, on this visit some of the Americans in the store were quite frankly loud and obnoxious, particularly when they began walking down the action figure aisle and using each figure as a starting point for a lengthy discussion about whether their push had been affected by wrestling politics.

It would be an exaggeration to say I walked away wanting to see somebody's face smashed in, but that wouldn't be a problem as the evening's show was from Big Japan. Again, it was a carefully-arranged buffet of styles with the first half having several junior-heavyweight matches and a Brahman Brothers waterfest before finishing with a barbed wire board death match (the 'appetiser' for the nights violent side.) During the interval, as a special treat, Abdullah Kobayashi walked up the aisles and signed autographs, making sure to press every sheet of paper into his bloody forehead to provide an extra souvenir.

The second half had something of a special attraction with Zero One's Kohei Sato and DDT's Shuji Ishikawa teaming up as the Twin Towers. On the same show last year, they had a classic with perennial Big Japan team Daisuke Sekimoto and Yuji Okabayashi. With Okabayashi out for as much as a year through shoulder injury, a replacement was needed for this 'rematch' and by now you can probably guess it was Hideki Suzuki, meaning I'd seen him in 10 matches in four days.

After a successful 'strong division' title defence by Daichi Hashimoto, it was time for the death match title with Masashi Takeda against Takumi Tsukamoto. Just the set-up process for this built the tension, with the ring crew removing the mat and padding to expose the bare boards, putting a nail-studded plank in one corner and a pile of chairs in the other, and then taping light tubes horizontally to cover every inch of ring ropes. Meanwhile everyone in the first couple of rows was given a sheet, which I thought was to guard them against flying blood but was also designed to shield them from debris. (That said the ring crew remained at ringside during the match and rushed into position to block any flying glass or chairs, which certainly takes 'paying your dues' to a new level.)

It's fair to say the match itself wouldn't appeal to everybody, but it definitely had an internal logic with the brutality ramping up so that every new stunt had more impact (physically and literally), and there was something satisfying to OCD tendencies in them making sure every light tube was broken and every available weapon used before they went to the finish. Without downplaying the physicality, the match was more about being spectacular than brutal, with the most shocking thing being just how loud the exploding light tubes are in person.

After the show I headed out to a venue that would surely be a high-scorer in the I SPY Tokyo Wrestling book, Ribera Steakhouse. For those who aren't familiar, it's a no-frills restaurant with nothing more than a small bench for customers to eat at, with the only real ordering decision being how big you want your flash-fried steak. Back in the 70s it became popular with touring Americans looking for somewhere open after shows and serving familiar food. This grew into a tradition with the owner filling the walls with pictures of wrestlers and presenting them with a branded jacket that wasn't available to buy and so became something of a badge of honour.

Ribera has two branches. The newer is just outside Shibuya and is more of a tourist attraction; the western fans I encountered who'd been there seemed to have a great time. The other branch is in Gotanda, a residential area that's a fair way out to the south of the city, meaning you're looking at a good 45-minute journey. Of course, it's worth the effort as this is the original and authentic Ribera steakhouse that's the only option if you want the true historic experience.

It's also closed for the best part of a week over New Year.

As you'd imagine, I was getting a little grumpy as I'd been starving myself most of the day so I could tackle the steak. Being so far out of town, it was also now too late to visit the 47 prefectures restaurant in Shibuya. With nothing else around in Gotanda, my only option was to head back to Korakuen where I had to try to find something to eat at almost 11pm. I decided that bare bones (perhaps literally) unfussy ramen was the way to go and made the mistake of asking Google Maps, which took me to a place just opposite my hotel called Jonathans.

Let's be honest, the English name and the sign describing it as a "Coffee & Restaurant" venue should have been a clue, but I was past the point of rational thought by now. The penny really started to drop when I leafed through the menu, complete with giant photographs and a range of what would best be described as international dishes including hamburger, fried chicken and even breakfasts with scrambled egg and sausages.

Yes, I had travelled 6,000 miles to one of the world's most diverse culinary hotspots and ended up in… Little Chef. Or at least its Japanese cousin.

To be fair, the food was decent enough (I went for a pork cutlet set), and it's open 24 hours with an option for unlimited soft drinks, meaning it's a good bet if you ever need to kill time overnight. But the (self-imposed) pressure was on to make tomorrow more worthy of culinary note.

Wednesday 3rd January

Had I wanted, I could have done another double at Korakuen Hall with the second half of an All Japan double-header and then whatever counts as a 'normal' DDT show. Instead I spent the day at Shin-Kiba 1st ring, a venue accessible by two trains and one subway route, in every case being figuratively and literally at the end of the line.

Shin-Kiba translates as "new lumberyard", which is appropriate given it's a largely industrial area. It's part of a series of man-made islands on reclaimed land bordering Tokyo Bay, and Shin-Kiba itself is mainly made up of warehouses and light industry designed for easy boat access. Skin-Kiba 1st RING is only three minutes' walk from the station and was a custom conversion to a wrestling arena in what is in effect a metal barn. It's very barebones (with the ticket desk and merchandise tables outside in a forecourt) but well-designed for wrestling with an intimate feel. There's a stage at one end, a couple of rows of seats on either side, and then at the other end a set of banked seating, albeit with solid benches rather than actual seats.

The lunchtime show was from an independent group called FREEDOMS and to be honest it all felt a little low rent -- which to be fair was literally the reason they run there. (The grimy atmosphere was also literal: every time the referee slapped the mat, dust came flying up.) Even without speaking Japanese, it was clear from the tone of a speech at the beginning that the wrestlers were trying to put across that they didn't have the resources of the major companies, but would make up for it with added effort or heart. (My notes for this section simply read "Indy as fuck.") Unfortunately ,that didn't pan out.

From the very first match it was clear the quality was significantly below that of anyone who'd run at Korakuen Hall. It wasn't so much that people were messing up moves or incompetent, but rather that there was a marked lack of intensity. Drew Galloway once recounted the story of the Undertaker telling him there was a difference between playing pro wrestler and being a pro wrestler, and I don't think I really understood that until I saw the difference between the tiers of promotions in Japan in such a concentrated manner.

I was left feeling very 'meh' by the first half, with a fellow named GENTARO standing out for the wrong reasons by being in black trunks and boots with a short haircut while failing to perform 'shoot style moves' smoothly. I christened him Shitbata and wish I'd had someone to share the joke with.

The theoretical highlight of the first half was a six-man tag that immediately broke down into an arena brawl, which was no doubt very exciting if you'd never seen such a thing in person before. (And hey, it was probably no worse than the eight-man tag match I raved about from the first time I went to an ECW show that didn't hold up on tape, but that was 22 years ago.) One team's entrance music played throughout the match in an obvious attempt to capture the chaotic feel of an ECW Gangstas match, but this was somewhat undermined when it continued while wrestlers were stood on the apron patiently waiting for a tag. Meanwhile two wrestlers attacked opponents with a pair of scissors and a screwdriver respectively. On the upside they were behaving responsibly in how they chose to wield the weapons, but on the downside they looked plain stupid by hitting their foes with the handles.

During the interval I passed up the opportunity to buy something from the extremely dubious food truck outside. (Though to be fair, Japanese tourists would be a lot more justified in complaining about the catering at one promotion I sometimes attend in the UK where you can be served tinned hot dog sausages retrieved from what appears to be a heated fish tank.) Instead I opted for a vending machine Kit Kat only to find it came in a cardboard box containing four miniature bars.

I also spotted a local wearing an FC Bristol hoodie, which certainly wasn't a team I recognised from my hometown. Some online research revealed it's actually a made-up team used so that a Japanese fashion label can produce 'branded' sportswear without having to worry about licensing issues.

Meanwhile a billboard across the street advertised kirakuen.com, which turned out to be a social housing group, but did lead me to find out that the correctly spelled "korakuen" literally translates as "paradise", which I couldn't really argue with.

Back in the underworld, Jun Kasai came out for a singles match and had a facial expression that could only be described as "I'm grumpy, I feel too old for this shit, but I'm still going to make the most of carving up myself and my opponent." It seemed oddly familiar, but I couldn't place it until I realised it was Mikey Whiplash to a tee. Then the show ended with GENTARO and another wrestler from earlier coming out again and between tiredness and not understanding the language, it took me far too long to grasp that this was a tournament final. Well, that and being distracted by one of the wrestlers at ringside wearing a hoodie of former Japanese boy band Sports Music Assemble People, but with "People" crossed out and replaced with "Motherfucker." (Insert the "We've Got a Badass Over Here" meme.)

It's only fair to mention that some people in the crowd clearly enjoyed the show, with a few of the tourists even thinking it was the best thing they'd seen all week. It also appeared that some of the Japanese fans go to FREEDOMS as an alternative to the bigger promotions. I later read an explanation that this was because of the cost, though that doesn't seem to make sense as the tickets were as expensive as most of the shows at Korakuen (and more so in a few cases.) As for me, I wouldn't say I regretted the experience, but it felt a lot like the level of show you'd go to in Britain five or ten years ago because you didn't have many chances to see live wrestling, but today is entirely skippable. And wherever it happened, there's no way in hell I'd pay £28 to see a show like this again.

I now had just under four hours to kill and it was clear Shin-Kiba was not going to occupy my attention for that long. I'd originally planned to take the train back to the 'mainland' and then walk over Rainbow Bridge, a landmark in its own right as well as a viewing point for Odaiba, a larger island that contains many of the futuristic buildings you'll see in shows and films set in Tokyo. Unfortunately, it was barely above freezing and windy, meaning being high and exposed would likely not have been a relaxing experience.

Instead I took the train back to Shibuya for a third attempt at the d47 restaurant. I found myself coming out of an exit I hadn't encountered before (which as we've established is not unusual in Tokyo), only to be slightly confused, turn 180 degrees, and find I was at the now familiar entrance to the tower containing the restaurant, albeit open for the first time. This led to the best part of 15 minutes of trying to get to the top of the tower that felt a bit like a frustrating level of a video game, at one point wandering round a balcony half-way up the building before figuring out that the only way to proceed was through several levels of a department store. (Again, it was less bad design and more extreme exhaustion.) Eventually I found the restaurant where I learned that – contrary to all guidebooks and website listings – they didn't serve food until the evening.

Fortunately, the tower had plenty of other restaurants of varying degrees of expense, novelty and dubious English translations. I wasn't compelled by "Rice people, Nice people!", didn't trust "Hakata horse horse" and was really not feeling alert enough to fully realise the potential of "GIRLS, BEERS, AMBITIOUS!" Instead I opted for Gyutan sumiyaki Rikyu and its description as "Store specializing in beef tongue charcoal grill."

This turned out to be underselling the establishment, which had an entire menu of dishes made from beef tongue. A far cry from the tinned pork tongue that Brits of a certain age will remember as a dubious treat in any picnic, beef tongue is hugely fatty and, in turn, utterly delicious when cooked in a suitable manner. While the grilled options were too much of a premium choice for my wallet, I opted for a Caesar salad where the beef replaces the usual chicken, followed by tongue slow braised in a red wine sauce. Chuck in an admittedly tiny portion of prosecco and the whole thing cost less than £14.

This meal also saw a miracle. After four decades I went to Japan still not quite getting my head around chopsticks (which will be no surprise to anyone who's seen the bizarre manner in which I hold a pen), and on the few meals I'd had so far with them on the trip it was pretty much a matter of survival. Here I was in a fairly high-end place, sat next to the the Japanese version of "ladies who lunch", trying to style it out and failing, to the point that the waiter brought over the cutlery of shame unprompted. I don't know if it was the tiredness, the lack of communication, or the indignation at my skills being challenged, but right at this moment it suddenly clicked in to place. The fork stayed untouched and the plate went back without a scrap of food left in place. I had prevailed.

Triumphantly I made my way through Shibuya in search of presents, taking a look at Tokyo Hands. It's the original store of a national chain, filling nine floors with, well, pretty much everything. It's almost like an old-fashioned department store (or for you younger readers, like a real-life version of Amazon) and while the emphasis is on creative hobbies, it's also got everything from 100 different models of umbrella to Cypriot salt to KISS moisturizing facepacks to earthquake survival kits.

I only made it up a couple of floors before having to head back over to Shin-Kiba for a Stardom show. With Wrestle Kingdom the next day, the show proved hugely popular with foreigners and it appeared the promotion didn't want to turn down any late requests for tickets. While the Big Japan show the day before probably had the highest raw number of non-Japanese fans (other than Wrestle Kingdom itself), this definitely had the highest proportion, with Westerners making up getting on for half the audience. The announced crowd was 445 and even if that was exaggerated, it was still an exceptionally tight fit in a building with an official capacity of 290. I was surprised to see Mark/Monkeybuckles stood behind my back row seat, not so much that he was at the show, but rather because nobody looking at the venue when empty would have concluded there was enough space for that to be a 'standing section'.

I suspect it was largely a combination of tiredness and high expectations based on reputation, but the show itself didn't really do it for me. Part of that was the format, with a five-match show, the last two being a six-woman and eight-woman tag respectively. While that seems to be a common Stardom set-up at smaller venues, it does mean the show was somewhat "top-heavy" talent-wise.

The show did mean I could adding Robbie & Xia Brookside to the short list of parent/child duos who I've both seen wrestle live, a sobering 22 years apart in this case. I also had a particularly bizarre moment when Delirious came out to announce Stardom's involvement in the ROH Women of Honor tournament. Those of you who enjoy a bit of Nordic Noir will likely have had the experience of being briefly baffled when the subtitles disappear and you think you've suddenly gained the ability to speak Danish, only to realise it's just that one of the characters is speaking English. I had much the same effect when, battling to stay awake, Delirious spoke and I could understand every word, realising embarrassingly late that this was because he wasn't doing his usual "speaking in tongues" gimmick.

Still, just in case I'd stopped doubting whether I was hallucinating, there was a spot in the main event where the heels held down one of the babyfaces, poured the contents of a packet of powdered soup mix into her mouth, then tipped a bottle of water over her face. I can only assume I looked particularly confused as one of the wrestlers involved, Kris Wolf, glanced over and shouted "Don't worry, it's just traditional Japanese shit!"

There wasn't much more to add to that and I decided to skip further exploration and instead head back to my room with pizza flavour crisps and mystery berry sweets for an early night, stopping only to do my freelance writing work. Having just taken Christmas off, I was still doing a couple of pieces a day for my North American tech news clients. This wasn't quite as simple as you'd expect as in local time my deadlines were now at 9pm and 2am respectively. That might sound super convenient, but the problem was that in most cases I was writing them much earlier in the day, and to save you doing the maths, let's just say I was having to write several days' news stories before the events concerned had happened...

Thursday 4th January

Perhaps the perfect example of the sheer ridiculousness of this trip was that it was the day of the biggest wrestling event of the year outside of WrestleMania, taking place 450 metres from my hotel, but I still stopped off at a show on the way.

Drawing (or negotiating) the best possible spot for passing trade was Tokyo Joshi Pro, which had 1,200 people in Korakuen Hall. It was a mirror image experience from that of Stardom as I knew nothing about the promotion and was pleasantly surprised. TJP is the women's branch of the DDT family and while the wrestling is perfectly fine, the emphasis is on colourful, distinctive characters. The only real disappointment was the show having the dull name of "Tokyo Women's Pro Wrestling '18" – the previous event there had been "We are starting to Korakuen again tighten the cord of the helmet" while the next show was listed as "let's go! Go! If you go! When you go! Get lost if you just go to Osaka!"

Among the highlights of the undercard were Veda Scott vs Maho Kurone – a battle explicitly worked as vegan vs zombie – and a special challenge by Maki Ito, who I later learned was low down the pecking order and had (in storyline) complained she wasn't getting a big enough challenge. The punchline was that her opponent was Danshoku Dino, who not only found his usual tactics of horrifying opponents with sexual advances didn't have any effect but was even the victim of unwanted kisses himself.

In the main bouts, Azusa Christie and Saki-sama stood out as a cool heel team, the tag title match of Shoko Nakajima and Yuka Sakazaki vs Mizuki and Riho was among the standouts of the week, and the main event of Miyu Yamashita vs Reika Saiki was a perfectly good bout, but I was most taken by the fact it was for the "TOKYO Princess Of Princess" championship.

The show ran fairly long, so there was less than an hour before the start of Wrestle Kingdom. I wandered over to look at the merchandise stand outside the Dome and discovered there was a queue just to get close enough to see the individual items. By the look of the queue there was a strong possibility I wouldn't get to the front by the time the show started.

That momentarily panicked me when I realised I still had to queue up to collect the ticket I'd bought on line, but in the event I simply walked straight up to a dedicated collection point and got it without delay, an impressive set-up given how many people had got their tickets through that route. In one of the weirder moments of my wrestling fandom, I used the spare time to hop on the free Tokyo Dome City Wi-Fi and buy tickets to see Will Ospreay in a Bristol school hall the following weekend.

Queuing up to get into the building itself I was seeing Western fans everywhere and conducted a quick survey by counting people going past until I'd tallied up 10 non-Japanese. It took 139, meaning seven percent were foreigners. Even dropping that down to five percent to account for the floor seats (reached from a separate queue) being much harder to buy from outside of Japan, you're still talking the best part of 2,000 visiting fans among the 35,000 crowd. To put that another way, there's a very strong chance that New Japan will draw more Americans to a single show – in Japan – than TNA does for any event in the US this year.

I felt confident taking my seat thanks to Google Translate's photo app, happily confirming to the person next to me that he was in the correct place. This inevitably led to more and more people checking with me until I started to panic that I might be responsible for an entire section's worth of people having to move...

I was at the front row of a block around half-way up the lower tier, giving plenty of legroom and a perfectly good view: to put the distance in perspective, I was splitting my gaze pretty much evenly between watching the ring itself and looking at the big screen for the fine detail.

One of the stranger insights into Japanese society came with a fan in a wheelchair who had enjoyed step-free access right to the front of our section only to find he was now expected to climb several steps to his row (and it wasn't quite clear where his chair was meant to go.) As the ushers looked on in bemusement, the person by the aisle on my row offered to swop seats, prompting a great deal of activity among the ushers that involved walkie talkies and the appearance of more senior staff. Initially I thought they were going to stop the swop and instead find a way to carry the man up to his correct seat. Instead it turned out that swopping seats was fine, but everyone involved had to fill out multiple forms and wait for the paperwork to be verified.

I'd feared that my section would be entirely filled with fans from overseas, but there was a good mix of travellers and locals, meaning I could see the reactions of native supporters. One Western fan was particularly loud and irritating with a constant stream of 'insider' commentary, but fortunately he decided to take a pew in a standing section out of earshot. Instead we got to hear the thoughts of a delightfully excited young Australian lad. During the four-way junior-heavyweight title match he exclaimed that "I'm going to tell everyone I know that I saw this!" It turned out he'd gone too early with his superlatives and as the Jericho-Omega match came to its conclusion, he was left with no option but to vow that "I'm going to tell everyone in the world that I saw this!"

The Dome itself is a wonderful venue to watch an event in, with great facilities. I got a perfectly satisfying beef curry and rice, served in a disposable dish clearly designed to be eaten at a stadium seat without risk of spillage, for the equivalent of £8. As well as the bars, you could get drinks at your seat from waitresses who continually switched between backpacks, each filled with a different drink served through the portable tapheads that pubs use for Coke and lemonade (and who wouldn't want jet-pumped whiskey.) And there was even a smoking room with TV screens to watch the action, though it's not clear how many people in there would have been able to see more than a few inches in front of their face given the wall-to-wall clouds of smoke.

As for the show itself, six hours (including the Rumble) didn't feel like a minute too long, though unfortunately Goto-Suzuki was the only match of the week were my (all-too-frequent) momentary lapses into slumber meant I missed a finish. Jericho-Omega absolutely felt like a co-main event worthy of its status. And the last few minutes of Naito-Okada were genuinely thrilling, with the Japanese fan next to me literally shaking in suspense. It does have to be said that the moment Okada got the three count, I was left without any doubt that Naito should have won, and around a third of the crowd (mainly clad in LIJ shirts) walked out almost immediately, but it was very much an atmosphere of disappointment rather than anger.

I had a relatively early start so headed straight home after the show, which ended around 10pm. There was one last demonstration of Japanese efficiency to come however. Everyone who'd entered via my gate – possibly as many as 5,000 people – had to exit through just three revolving doors. Yet by having staff turn the doors themselves at a steady pace and directing people through at exactly the right speed so that the doors never stopped moving, everyone was out in just a few minutes.

Friday 5th January

Despite checking out of my hotel at 10am, my flight wasn't until a frankly ludicrous 2.45am. The good news was that as well as having a chance to do some proper tourist stuff, I'd still be able to go to a show in Shinjuku on the way to the airport, taking the final total to 14 shows in eight days. While leaving the hotel I picked up a copy of a daily sports newspaper that had a three-and-a-half page report on Wrestle Kingdom as its lead story.

First on the tourist trail was Ginza, which is a mix of business district and boutique shopping area. I took the opportunity to put my bag in a subway station locker (having been too terrified to risk leaving it in Shinjuku station and never finding the lockers again), stopping to read a sign that certainly raised questions about the events that inspired it. It depicted a young woman giving up her seat to an elderly man with the predictable caption "How nice of you to offer" and then the wonderfully passive-aggressive reply "Hearing 'Thank you' is nice too."

I spent most of the next hour wandering around trying to find a restaurant called Ginza Steak, which was somewhat challenging given Ginza is an area known for its steak restaurants. The main problem was that the restaurant website's directions used a subway exit (of which, we have established, there are many) as a reference point. Presumably it would have spoiled the upscale effect by giving the more useful information that it's right behind Hooters.

During my search I came across a statue of Godzilla – or rather the scaffolding and fencing that hid the statue to protect it from construction work – and the baffling sight of a restaurant that was pushing an allegedly gourmet dish that these Western eyes recognised instantly as a sausage roll.

I made the restaurant just in time and was pleasantly surprised to find that, having booked the all-you-can-eat lunch special, I was taken up to the chef's private kitchen area where I sat around the hot-plate grill with around 10 other guests, all Japanese. This proved reassuring as I was able to simply take my cue from my neighbour etiquette-wise. Well, until I blew it by choosing the "plum wine-whiskey-sake soda cocktail" from the drinks menu and the waitress having to patiently explain I had to choose one of the spirits…

It was a multi-course affair, kicking off with a mushroom salad, a soup with dried mullet roe, and then "teppan-steamed Shabu", which I was particularly intrigued about given the Internet reliably informed me Shabu was local slang for methamphetamine. In reality it was a small meat and vegetable stew put into a pot on the grill to steam.

Tasty and elegant as it was, I was here for the main event, the "time-limited trial course" of wagyu beef. Wagyu refers to four specific breeds of cattle from Japan, with particularly delicious characteristics. They have high levels of amino acids, which is the main source of the umami (or 'meaty') flavour in a steak. They also have a high fat content of up to 25 percent compared with just a couple of percent in most steaks. The fat is streaked throughout the steak, almost like streaky bacon, giving it a marbled look. This fat is key not only because it gives the mouth-watering texture, but because it carries the flavour of the meat around your tongue. Because it's marbled, you don't get the split between dry meat and tough fat that you get in many steaks: instead every bite is juicy.

If you're wondering if this is the same as Kobe beef, the Kobe name is reserved for meat that comes from one of the wagyu breeds, is produced in a specific area of Japan, and meets several other criteria. It's the most expensive form of wagyu beef and the type of dish you take out a second mortgage for. That's not to say I wasn't having the good stuff. The restaurant only uses A5 grade wagyu, which means both the meat and the fat receive the highest "superior" classifications for colour, texture and lustre. It's absolutely a very special occasion meal, bordering on 'an experience' even for Japanese natives.

The cooking process simply consists of taking bite-sized chunks and searing them, which is partly to give the meat just enough texture that it doesn't collapse when picked up with chopsticks, and partly to start melting the fat, which has a particularly low melting point. When you put it into your mouth, even the pressure from your tongue and the warmth of your mouth is enough to collapse it into what's almost a sauce. Perhaps the easiest way to imagine it is if you could extract all the meaty taste from a full-sized steak and somehow deliver it in a knob of butter.

I managed three platefuls (perhaps 600 grams altogether) before it started to feel like overload and of course being competitive, noted my credible upper mid-table performance among the guests in the room. Only one diner had to have the time limit enforced and, as you might guess, it was the slenderest, most delicate young girl.

After resorting to gestures to stop the beef coming, I was given the last couple of courses of "corned beef rice soup" and an ice cream. The former was the final undoing of any pretence at sophistication I might have pulled off: after taking care of the slivers of raw wagyu on top, I was left with a bowl of rice collapsed in a beef broth, and let's just say my new-found chopstick competence did not expand that far. All told the meal cost a little over £50 and was utterly worthwhile as my one real extravagance of the trip.

After stopping off at a joyous gift shop full of utter, utter tat (in which I bought a box of "purple sweet potato" Kit-Kats), I took the train up to Akihabara, known colloquially as 'Electric City'. This was the place to go if you wanted the stereotypical picture of Japan as futuristically weird. The only way I could describe its mix of shops and characters was if Maplin opened a massage parlour on Blackpool seafront. It's certainly the only place I've ever seen street hawkers slide up and surreptitiously offer to sell you a USB cable out of a carrier bag.

Probably the closest thing to a genuinely unsettling experience happened here when, having got a taste for iced coffee during the week, I bought one from a vending machine. Not only was it in a can, but it turned out to be milky, sugary, and close to boiling temperature. It was a surprise to my mouth, though one that quickly drew attention to the fact my hand was about to scald on the metal surface.

I also got to see a modern twist on classic teenage behaviour. The familiar sight of two boys on their first trip to the big city messing about at the entrance to what was clearly a sex club or massage parlour, both pretending to push the other one in the door, was accompanied by the more contemporary sight of another of their friends surreptitiously live-streaming their antics on an iPad.

Walking down one back street I saw a sign for 'Bodydrop' and took the gamble that it was worth climbing five flights of stairs. It turned out it was indeed a wrestling shop, or at least a section of a toy shop dedicated to wrestling figures, DVDs and shirts. It was no Toudoukan, but it did have a few neat novelties such as a Money In The Bank briefcase complete with a replica of the 'contract' that's supposedly inside. There was also a reminder of just how wide New Japan's current range of merchandise is, the most outlandish being a shirt celebrating Bad Luck Fale destroying Daryl the cat.

Things turned weirder on the main street. I wasn't too surprised to see one of Tokyo's maid cafes where people pay large amounts of cash to be served drinks by women in said fancy dress. However, I was thrown by a large billboard advertising the upcoming release of a maid simulator video game, not just because of the subject, but because the list of platforms included Windows 98. For all its futurism, there's some parts of Japanese society and technology that seem bizarrely dated, not least the fact that manufacturing Filofaxes appears to still be a viable business.

I also stopped in at a five-storey video arcade where I felt every bit of my age. Most memorable was the top floor which houses the rhythm games, covering everything from dancing to drumming to jabbing at the screen to try to keep an anime movie playing. It's the only place I've been that has more electronic noise than the casinos of Vegas.

I then popped back to Shibuya to complete my trek round Tokyo Hands in search of a present. Everything was in the gap between genuinely desirable and ironically kitsch (I settled on a Bento lunchbox), but the guidebook's warning that "you can lose hours in there" proved correct. Unfortunately, this meant I didn't have time to visit Antonio Inoki's recently-opened themed bar in Shinjuku, though to make up for it Tokyo Hands did have a 2018 calendar for the man himself, complete with the cheesy poses you might expect on a similar production for, say, Cliff Richard.

Shinjuku was my final destination, specifically Shinjuku Face. It's on the seventh floor of an entertainment complex and is a former gig venue that's been converted to a custom-built combat sports venue. It's the upscale version of Shinkiba 1st-Ring with a built-in bar area and comfortable banked seating. While it can house 500 or so people, it's incredibly intimate: I was in the back row, but still within 10 feet or so of the ring.

My farewell entertainment was a DDT show, which opened with a four-way tag match that was all about Joey Ryan. Yes, he did the penis spots, but he also had a non-stop barrage of banter, starting when the ring crew began clearing up the streamers and he threw a tantrum, insisting he be allowed to keep them as they were meant as a present. Between that and some unspeakable behaviour with a lollipop, he dominated the focus of the match, and yet I don't think he left his feet once.

Opener aside, this was a very different show to the previous DDT offerings. It was the opening night of the D-King tournament, the promotion's take on the G-1 Climax. That meant six 'straight' singles matches with the top serious wrestlers in the promotion. Everything was solid, the second half was a triple treat, and the David vs Goliath clash of Shuji Ishikawa and Mike Bailey may well have been the best non-New Japan match I saw all week.

With the show done by barely 9pm, I had plenty of time to go and retrieve my luggage, which proved fortunate as I struggled to get my day's shopping into it. And by "struggled" I mean that Friday night revellers on the subway were greeted by the sight of an increasingly-flustered Westerner sat in the entrance lobby in a 15-minute-plus battle to close the zip without breaking it, including at one stage squatting on to the case to apply my full bodyweight.

Once that debacle was complete, it was a simple monorail trip out to Haneda Airport (which is a far closer alternative to the more popular Narita) where I not only got rebooked to an aisle seat, but was told that because of the late hour, we were allowed to use the airline lounge usually reserved for premium passengers. This was a magnificent experience that left me wondering if I could cope with ordinary departure lounges again. We're talking a choice of massage chairs or one-person sofas arranged for maximum privacy, complete with ample power sockets and high-speed wireless broadband. We're talking a buffet with hot food and snacks. And we're talking an unlimited bar where the only hassle was choosing between champagne because, well, it's champagne, or beer because you get to put your glass in the hand of a robotic pouring arm.

Suffice to say I was exceptionally relaxed in my sofa with a glass of bubbles, watching New Year's Dash on my laptop. That peacefulness was sorely interrupted when a child kicked the back of my sofa exceptionally hard. I turned around to find the culprit was clearly hiding and as I scanned the room, I could see that other passengers were clearly put out on my behalf at such disruptive behaviour.

Well, that's what I thought at first. Then I realised it had been an earthquake.

Fortunately, it was only a "small to moderate" quake that didn't cause any lasting damage and it was soon time to board the plane. The main excitement here was discovering that the in-flight entertainment included two matches from New Japan Pro Wrestling. This started with Riki Choshu vs Genichiro Tenyru from the 1993 Tokyo Dome show, which was shocking for just how little they actually did in the match by today's standards. (I should note that hearing my mother-in-law attempt to say "Genichiro Tenyru" when reading my mention of this in my FSM trip report was something of a life highlight.)

The rest of the show was the Omega-Naito G-1 Climax final from 2017, which naturally seemed ridiculously fast-paced in comparison. After a while I realised this wasn't just a comparative issue. Crunching the numbers, I realised the 34-minute match had been sped up so that it took up a 22-minute slot on the video. I took this as my cue to attempt sleep.

After a final 12 hours in the company of exceptionally polite, professional, warm and helpful service staff, I arrived at Heathrow and completed the seemingly endless walk to the bus station as the travellators were out of action. Here I was met at the desk by a rude, dismissive 'customer service' worker who clearly didn't want to be here, let alone pretend to answer a question without expressing contempt for humanity.

My time in Japan was over.

Tokyo Travel Guide

If I've done my job writing this book, you'll be ready to make your own trip to Tokyo. While there's no shortage of guidebooks for Japan or Tokyo, they understandably aren't tailored to wrestling voyages, so I've put together some of the most useful guidelines from my own experience.

What's It Going To Cost?

There's no easy way round this: a wrestling trip to Tokyo is going to be an expensive proposition for most Western fans. As a guideline, my flight from London was £800, my hotel was just under £400 for seven nights, and I spent 53,180 yen (£356) on tickets to shows.

To be honest, there really isn't much scope for cutting down on these costs without it being a false economy. Unfortunately, the prime periods for Japanese wrestling (new year, summer and the cherry blossom season) are also peak travel times. In my case I could have saved around £200 on flight costs by taking an indirect flight. It's really down to your attitude and budget, but when you're talking 12 hours to start with, I found it worth the extra cash to avoid an even longer journey and the stress of making connections.

With hotel costs, you could find a cheaper part of Tokyo, but I'd definitely advise staying within walking distance of Tokyo Dome City if you can. This gives you the option of going back to your hotel in the afternoon if you're doing a double-header and either you're tired or the weather is bad. AirBnB is an option, though I'd probably not do this until a second trip when you're a bit more familiar with the locations and culture, so would be better able to adjust if there's any problem. I stayed at the Wing Korakuen while Tokyo resident Martin Walton recommends the Sakura Hotel in nearby Jimbocho as an economy alternative. He also notes that if you're on a very tight budget you could try the Green Plaza and Kuyakusho-ma capsule hotels in Shinjuku.

For the wrestling tickets, I generally went for the cheapest available reserved seating, which was mainly around 3,000 to 4,000 yen (£21 to £28). With Korakuen Hall and particularly with the smaller venues, you're going to get a perfect view wherever you are, so you'd really have to want to sit ringside for it to be worth paying extra. (I did avoid unreserved seating where that was an option, simply because the language barrier could be a problem in figuring out where you could or could not sit.)

For the Tokyo Dome I got a 1F (lower tier) seat for 9,000 yen (£63). The only other option readily available was the upper tier, which really is a long way from the ring.

Obviously, you don't have to go to 14 shows in a week, particularly if you want to do a lot of sightseeing. My only advice here would be to go to as many different promotions as you can and take a chance on those you don't know, rather than regret missing out when you return home.

Food and drink and other day-to-day costs are cheaper than you might expect and sometimes less than you'd pay in many British cities. Wagyu beef aside, I generally paid a few hundred yen for snacks, around 700-1,000 yen (£5-7) for food court meals, and around 2,000 yen (£14) for table service restaurant meals with a beer or wine.

Transport (detailed below) cost me around 6,500 yen (£43) including airport transfers and subway/train tickets.

How Do I Get Tickets?

To find out what shows are on during your visit, check out en.puwota.com. This English language site lists most shows: click on the ticket icon for a direct link to the PIA ticket agency website (see below) or click on the time and venue in the listing to go to the relevant page on the promotion's website.

I probably used every means possible to get tickets to shows, partly to spread out any risks and partly to minimize the amount of cash I had to take with me. Here are the options I used:

- Korakuen Hall

You have two options with Korakuen Hall. Between 9am and 5pm (possibly not at weekends) you can buy tickets at the box office on the fifth floor for any shows other than those happening the same day. It's a fairly straightforward process as you just need to say/show which event you want tickets for and then point to your chosen seat on a plan.

The other option is to buy from the ticket window outside the building, which opens a few hours before each show. It has clear signs showing when it opens, what show is on sale and what tickets are available. (A cross means that category of tickets is unavailable; a circle means tickets are available.) You'll be able to buy any unsold seats, along with standing balcony tickets, which are only sold on the day of a show.

It's worth noting that even the busiest show I went to at Korakuen Hall still had some empty seats, so it's highly likely you'll be able to get everything you need from a trip to the box office in advance. That means the only real need to buy in advance is for peace of mind or to cut down on the amount of cash you need to bring with you.

The big exception is New Japan which always sells out these days and for which the balcony is likely your only shot. The queue starts ridiculously early, though I'm told you can reserve your place in line by taping down a sheet of newspaper on which you've written your name and how many tickets you want to buy.

- Reservations

Several promotions allow you to reserve tickets and pick them up at the door. (It's worth writing your name on a piece of paper so they can find the relevant envelope more easily.) This can be via the promotion's website or by email. When using websites, Google Translate (either by right-clicking in Chrome or installing the relevant extension) is a real life-saver.

DDT: I got mine from Diego a. I don't know if he is still able to do this, though I also have rekka.tw@gmail.com listed as doing reservations.

Gatoh Move: http://gatohmove.com/?page_id=169

Note that once you use Google Translate, there's one field in the form reading "mail address" and another reading "E-mail address (confirmation)". In fact, you need to put your email address in both fields. It's pick up and pay at the venue.

Ice Ribbon: http://iceribbon.com/ticket_list.php

Stardom: stardom@friend.ocn.ne.jp

- Online Purchases

Big Japan has online ticket sales at http://bjw.shop-pro.jp/. You'll need to create an account giving your hotel details for the address and phone number and then make sure to select the reserved seats/pick up option rather than have them mailed. For Korakuen Hall events, it's worth checking Japanican.com as you may be able to get a discount deal.

All Japan tickets are available through https://www.confetti-web.com/en/guide/flow_index.php and can be picked up from any Tokyo 7/11.

ePlus is a ticket agency that's generally not too easy to use for overseas visitors. However, New Japan arranged a special English language page for ordering for Wrestle Kingdom (collecting at the Tokyo Dome box office with a passport as ID) and looks set to do the same for other major events. You'll find details at njpw1972.com.

http://ticketpay.jp/ carries some promotions' tickets and you can pay online and then pick up at a Lawson's convenience store. As noted previously, this is not the easiest process so is probably only worthwhile if it's the only option for a show at a smaller venue.

Pia.jp is arguably the biggest ticket site and is also a good backup for picking up any shows Puwota has missed. To check here, copy the Japanese symbols for "puroresu" (which you'll find on the Wikipedia page for puroresu) into the search box. From the list of results you'll be able to filter down to the specific dates you are visiting. In theory you can buy online here and then pick up at a convenience store, but this is quite hit and miss and can be tricky with non-Japanese bank cards. A better bet is to print out the event page and then take it to one of the several PIA desks in the arrivals lobbies at Narita Airport. Do be aware that some events come off sale through PIA a day or two before the show.

Finally, you'll find several companies that specialise in buying goods from Japanese shops and shipping them overseas. While these companies can and do buy event tickets, I checked a few and the fees were excessively high to the point that in some case you'd be paying double the price of the ticket.

Transport: Overview

Getting around Tokyo on public transport is very easy, despite the maps appearing terrifyingly busy. Multiple operators run subway and overground trains, but fortunately you really don't need to worry about who does what. For the vast majority of travel within Tokyo, the subway will work fine.

To make life even easier get the official Tokyo Subway app (which doesn't need an internet connection to work) as this will tell you the quickest route between any stations and the relevant connections plus the total cost. Even if you forget the names of stations or lines, all you really need to follow is the line colour and station number. Unlike the London Underground, you can almost always go in both directions from the same platform, so you just need to make sure you pick the side with the numbers going in the right direction. If you do ever lose track while on the train, the station number is almost always visible at each stop.

(One pitfall to watch out for is that the last stop on a subway line isn't always the last stop for the train. Some trains follow the subway line but then carry on at the end and become overground commuter trains.)

The overground trains work as well or better, but can be harder to navigate. My rule of thumb would be that if you are going directly between two locations with stations on the Yamamote Line (a circular overground route that's an unofficial border of central Tokyo), use the train as it's quicker. Otherwise, the subway will be easiest.

Note that the last train on many lines is around 11-11.30pm, so you'll need to plan ahead and possibly take another route if you're returning late.

Transport: Venues and routes

The stations for the main wrestling venues are as follows:

Korakuen Hall/Tokyo Dome: Korakuen station (station N11 on the Namboku/light green line or M22, Maranouchi/red line) or Suidiobashi station (I11, Mita/dark blue line or Chuo overground line.)

Shin-Kiba 1st Ring: Shin-Kiba station (Y24, Yurakucho/dark yellow line, or Keiyo and Rinkai overground lines)

Ryōgoku Kokugikan aka Sumo Hall: Ryogoku station (E12, Oedo/pink line, or Sobu overground line)

Budokan Hall: Kundanshita Station (S05, Shinjuku/dark green line or Z06, Hanzomon/purple line or T07, Tozai/light blue line

Ichigaya Chocolate Plaza: Ichigaya station (S04, Shinjuku/dark green line or Y14, Yurakucho/dark yellow line or N09, Namboku/light green line)

For **Shinjuku Face**, you've got multiple options as Shinjuku is served by several subway and overground lines and stations that you can walk between without coming out to the street. Once you're in the complex:

- follow signs for the East exit to get you in the right part of the station (you may need to go downstairs);
-
- then look specifically for exit B13.
-

Most show times should leave you plenty of time to get between venues. If you're in a rush the best bets are:

Ichigaya-Korakuen Hall: two stops on the Shinjuku/dark green line (10 to 15 minutes total)

Budokan Hall to Korakuen Hall: 15 to 20 minute walk

Ryōgoku Kokugikan to Korakuen Hall: Chuo-Sobu overground line between Ryogoku and Suidobashi then walk to Korakuen (15 minutes total)

Transport: Payments

Read any guidebook and you'll likely see a recommendation for the Japan Rail Pass. Simply put, if you're not going to be leaving Tokyo, forget about it as it won't be worth the money. (If you are going on any long train trip to another city, it likely will.)

You can buy tickets for individual journeys, but the easiest option is an IC card. It's the Tokyo equivalent of London's Oyster card in that you top it up with cash and tap it at the barriers when you enter and exit a station. Unlike the London Underground, you also need to tap out and in when you change lines. The barrier has an electronic display shows how much the journey cost and how much you have left on the card.

There's two types of IC card called Suica and Pasmo, which you can buy at stations (including at the airports) from vending machines and some shops. Within Tokyo, Suica and Pasmo are effectively interchangeable and which you get will depend on who operates the station or machine where you buy it.

You pay 2,000 yen to buy the card, of which 500 yen is a deposit, leaving you with a 1,500 yen balance. You can top this up in machines at any station in any amount as and when you need to. If you don't have enough left on your card to pay for a journey you won't be able to get out of the ticket barrier at the destination. However, you simply go to a nearby 'fare adjustment' machine to add the necessary balance to your card.

In theory you can return the card and get a refund of the 500 yen deposit and any unspent balance (minus a withdrawal fee). However, you need to go to a manned ticket booth operated by the same company/area as the machine or station where you bought it, so this usually isn't worth the hassle.

The beauty of the IC cards is that they work on almost all forms of subway and overground train (including the monorail to Haneda Airport but not the express trains to Narita) without you having to worry about who operates a line.

One alternative to an IC card is a day-long unlimited subway pass. This is only really worth doing if you'll be making at least four long journeys on the same day, and you'll need to make sure you get one that covers all the lines rather than the cheaper option that only covers one operator. In practice, the small savings really aren't worth the extra hassle.

Transport: Other options

Taxis are expensive and you may need to show your destination written down in Japanese. As far as I can tell, if you already have an Uber account and app, this works without any reconfiguration. Again, it's expensive, but there's no late-night surcharge, so it could be a useful safety net if you miss the last train. If it comes to it, most major roads have well-lit pavements (sidewalks), so if you've got a decent navigation app, walking isn't the utter no-no that it would be in some cities.

Money

Japan is largely a cash society and you shouldn't rely on being able to use a debit or credit card anywhere. If you need to use a cash machine/ATM, Western cards won't work everywhere. They should work in the machines in a 7/11, but the one I used had a 10,000 yen minimum withdrawal, so plan ahead.

The smallest banknote is 1,000 yen, so you'll wind up with a lot of change in coins, and the colour/size of the different denominations isn't as logical as you might hope. Most are marked with the amount, so you simply need to remember that the silver one with a hole is 50 yen and the gold one with a hole is 5 yen.

To avoid cluttering up your pockets, I'd suggest taking out all the 5 and 1 yen coins each day and putting them aside as you'll rarely need them for vending machines or shop purchases. The only place they are really of use is in 100 yen stores as the sales tax isn't included, so each item actually costs 108 yen.

Jetlag

If you're flying from Europe to Tokyo, there's no way round the fact that you are going to encounter some of the worst possible jetlag, arriving "three hours before you leave" but a day later. (Those in the Americas will more likely get problems coming home.) In my experience, it wasn't really the "day or two of zombieness before settling down" that I'd expected, but rather my sleep pattern feeling completely randomised for the best part of the week. While I'd go with the usual jetlag advice (sleep on the plane if you can; try to stay awake until a normal local bedtime on the day you arrive; don't use alcohol as a sleep inducer), after the first day I'd say to get sleep whenever you can, including afternoon naps, and not stress yourself out too much about being awake at nighttime.

Solo travel

Whether travelling across the world to an unfamiliar culture is something you want to do alone depends largely on your personality. The main disadvantage I found is that you have to be comfortable with the idea of possibly going entire days without having a conversation in English. (That said, if you're travelling at New Year at least, it's very easy to find other Western wrestling fans, and the "NJPW Wrestle Kingdom 12 Travel Group" on Facebook looks set to stick around even though the event has now passed.)

The upside is that you get more flexibility with your schedule, particularly in coping with fluctuating energy levels.

For what it's worth, I didn't encounter any situations with restaurants or other activities where being on my own caused any problems. The only real exceptions might be in some table service bars at busy times.

Technology

Coming from the UK, you can use a UK-US adaptor for Japanese sockets. However, you need one which just has the two flat pins and doesn't have the third round (earth) pin. These can be tricky to find at airports, so it's worth getting one beforehand.

Japan is on 100 volts. That's fine for USB adaptors. If you're taking a laptop, check the label on the power lead/adaptor to make sure it can cope with 100 volts. (In reality, if your adaptor only goes as low as 110 volts, it should be fine.)

Check your hotel's website or online reviews to see if it specifically lists internet access as being Wi-Fi. If not, it may be Ethernet only. If so, you can buy USB-Ethernet adaptors if you need one for your laptop, though you may be out of luck with phones.

Public Wi-fi is hit and miss at best, so it's well worth getting some form of mobile Internet, if only for the security and convenience of maps (Google doesn't have the rights to let users download maps of Tokyo, so Google Maps won't work without a data connection.) I went for a pre-paid SIM from econnectjapan.com which cost 2,138 yen (around £14) for 500 MB and was valid for 7 days. As long as you're just using it to check information and directions rather than extensive browsing and social media updates, this should be enough data. Unlike some services, I didn't have to return the card at the end of the week.

An alternative is to hire a pocket Wi-fi device, which takes a mobile data signal and rebroadcasts it as a Wi-Fi network. The upside is you don't have to worry about compatibility with your phone but the downside is it's one more thing to carry round and keep charged, plus you'll often have to return it in person or by post, which may not be convenient.

If you do need Wi-Fi at and around shows, there's a decent signal (free with registration) outside the Tokyo Dome and Korakuen Hall, though it doesn't stretch inside Korakuen Hall itself. Mobile internet works inside both venues.

Language

If you really want to learn Japanese before going, I'd recommend hunting down something like the BBC Active Talk Japanese course. It uses CDs and a book and is designed to take 10 weeks, with around a one-hour 'lesson' once a week and then 10-15 minutes revision each day. However, you do need to stick with this: I had to stop about halfway through when life got unexpectedly busy and had lost a lot of what I'd learned by the time I got to Japan.

It's also worth being prepared for the fact that no matter how well you learn, jetlag could mean it's hard enough speaking in English for a few days, let alone Japanese, plus it's a struggle to overcome some instincts. For example, if somebody says "hai" ("yes") to you, don't beat yourself up for saying "hi" back without thinking.

In reality, you can get by with a very limited Japanese vocabulary. This is partly because a lot of signs are in English and many service staff will be able to speak some basic English, and partly because it's surprising just how much you can understand and communicate through pointing, gestures and assessing tone and context (and not worrying about looking stupid.)

Here's the vocabulary that I found genuinely worth knowing during my trip:

"Ohayo gozaimasu", "konnichi wa" and "konban wa" are "good morning", "good afternoon" and "good evening" respectively.

"Arigato" is "thank you" and you can extend to "arigato gozaimasu" if you need to emphasise particular gratitude.

"Sumimasen" is roughly equivalent to "excuse me" but can cover anything from getting somebody's attention, to asking them to let you squeeze past, to apologising for a collision.

If you can't find your assigned seat, pointing to the relevant information on the ticket while saying "doko desu ka?" is the simplest (if grammatically questionable) way to ask for help.

"Moshi moshi" is something you might hear from staff when walking into a shop. It roughly translates as "I am acknowledging your presence" and doesn't require a response other than a polite smile.

"...o kudasai" after something means "please can I have...", for example when ordering in a restaurant.

"Shiteiseki" (prounounced stay-sekki) is "reserved seat".

Numbers are very simple:

One = ichi

Two = ni

Three = san

Four = yon (*)

Five = go

Six = roku

Seven = nana

Eight = hachi

Nine = kyu

Ten = ju.

(* - Four can also be said as "shi", though this is usually only done when counting. It's the same sound as the word for "death", which creates a superstition similar to 13 in our culture and is why a fourth floor may be 'missing' in buildings.)

Everything up to one hundred simply combines the numbers. For example, 14 is ju-yon while 57 is go-ju-nana.

If you need to go higher, "hyaku" is a hundred. The same "put the digits together" principle applies, so 223 is ni-hyaku-ni-ju-san. The only real exceptions are that 600 is said as rop-pyaku and 800 as hap-pyaku, in both cases because it flows better. A thousand is "sen" and again you simply build up the words to make the relevant number.

The only real exception you need to know with numbers is that there's a different system for indicating quantities. To ask for one of something is "hitotsu", two is "futatsu", three is "mittsu" and four is "yottsu".

For example, "hitotsu shiteseki o kudasai" is what you'd say at the Korakuen Hall ticket window to get one reserved seat for that day's show.

The simplest rule for pronunciation is to stress each syllable equally and say the whole word a little slower than you would in English. Many words are either the same or close in English, so it can be worth giving the English word a shot if you're stuck. For the most part, Japanese syllables are pronounced as you'd expect, though with 'su' the 'u' is virtually silent.

Finally, I'd highly recommend the Google Translate app as you can take a photo of a sign or ticket and it will detect and translate Japanese writing. You can even download the Japanese dictionary so it will work without an internet connection. Realistically it's not worth trying to learn Japanese symbols before travelling, though it would be useful to learn or print out the symbols for North, South, East and West to help you find seats.

For The Record: The Full Results

Wave Great Year End Thanksgiving WAVE '17, Korakuen Hall, 29/12/17 (attendance 783)

Fairy Nihonbashi/Hikaru Shida/Kaori Yoneyama/Miyuki Takase 2-1 Cherry/Mio Momono/Moeka Haruhi/Sakura Hirota

Mio Momono p Fairy Nihonbashi

Fairy Nihonbashi p Mio Momono

Miyuki Takase p Sakura Hirota

Mika Iida bt Hiroe Nagahama (5:12)

Kenichiro Arai/Masayuki Mitomi bt Keisuke Goto/Koji Takeda (11:26)

Hardcore: Rina Yamashita/Ryo Mizunami bt KAORU/SAKI (15:22)

NEW-TRA (Rin Kadokura/Takumi Iroha) bt Nagisa Nozaki/Yuki Miyazaki (18:00)

Chihiro Hashimoto/Meiko Satomura bt ASUKA/Ayako Hamada

Yumi Ohka bt Misaki Ohata to win Regina Di WAVE Title

DDT DAMNATION Produce Illegal Gathering Vol 2, Korakuen Hall, 30/12/17 (attendance 1,050)

Gauntlet Costume Change Battle Royal: HARASHIMA bt Ken Ohka, Man Man Kai Kind, Ryuichi Sekine, Saki Akai, Soma Takao, Takayuki Ueki, Yuki Ueno (14:04)

Dick Togo/Guanchulo bt Antonio Honda/Colt Cabana (13:40)

(Togo beat Guanchulo for DDT Iron Man Heavy Metal Title during match)

KO-D Six Man champions Shuten Doji (KUDO/Masahiro Takanashi/Yukio Sakaguchi) bt Mad Paulie (Nobuhiro Shimatani)/Mad Paulie (Ryota Hama)/Mad Paulie (9:36)

Violent Giants (Shuji Ishikawa/Suwama) bt Brahman Brothers (Brahman Kei/Brahman Shu)

Masashi Takeda/Tetsuya Endo bt Konosuke Takeshita/Masato Tanaka (15:35)

Hardcore match: Yuko Miyamoto 2-1 Daisuke Sasaki to win DDT Extreme Title (29:43)

Big Japan Wrestling, Korakuen Hall, 30/12/17 (attendance 1,133)

Kazumi Kikuta bt Masaki Morihiro (6:59)

Speed Of Sounds (Hercules Senga/Tsutomu Oosugi) bt Brahman Kei/Brahman Shu (5:47)

Ryota Hama/Yasufumi Nakanoue bt Kota Sekifuda/Tatsuhiko Yoshino (6:55)

Daisuke Sekimoto bt Yuya Aoki (11:07)

Kazuki Hashimoto/Kohei Sato bt Hideki Suzuki/Takuya Nomura (8:14)

Ryuichi Kawakami/Yoshihisa Uto bt Okami (Daichi Hashimoto/Hideyoshi Kamitani) (11:32)

BJW Junior Heavyweight champion Shinobu bt Kankuro Hoshino (13:43)

Death Battle Royal: Abdullah Kobayashi beat Great Kojika, Isami Kodaka, Jaki Numazawa, Kenji Fukimoto, Masaya Takahashi, Minoru Fujita, Ryuichi Sekine, Ryuji Ito, Takayuki Ueki, Toshiyuki Sakuda & Yuko Miyamoto (24:17)

Ice Ribbon #858 RibbonMania 2017, Korakuen Hall, 31/12/17 (attendance, 1,235)

Tsukasa Fujimoto bt Tsukushi (9:53)

Elimination: Julia/Karen DATE/Satsuki Totoro bt Hana DATE/Ibuki Hoshi/Mammoth Ineko (12:49)

Hamuko Hoshi/Matsuya Uno/Mochi Miyagi bt Makoto/Maya Yukihi/Tequila Saya (11:05)

Hardcore: Arisa Nakajima bt Akane Fujita (10:23)

Hideki Suzuki bt Miyako Matsumoto (0:06)

Hideki Suzuki bt Miyako Matsumoto (0:05)

Hideki Suzuki bt Miyako Matsumoto (6:28)

Kyuri/Maika Ozaki bt Saori Anou/Tae Honma (10:56)

Young Ice Tournament Final: Nao DATE bt Maruko Nagasaki (8:06)

Hiragi Kurumi bt Risa Sera (13:33) to win ICExInfinity Title

Gatoh-Move 331, Ichigaya Chocolate Plaza, 31/12/17 (attendance 76)

Chango p Balliyan Akki (6:24)

Masahiro Takanashi d Choun Shiryu (10:00)

Emi Sakura/Obihiro Sayaka/Saki p Toru Owashi/Riho/Mitsuru Konno (10:55)

DDT/Big Japan, Toshikoshi Pro Wrestling 2017 – Toshiwasure! Two Organization Shuffle Tag Tournament, Korakuen Hall, 31/12/17 (attendance 1,411)

R1: Daisuke Sekimoto/Kazusada Higuchi bt Ryota Hama/Soma Takao (6:06)

R1: Akito/Kazuki Hashimoto bt Kota Sekifuda/Ryota Nakatsu (4:32)

R1: Brahman Shu/Daisuke Sasaki bt Antonio Honda/Takuya Nomura (7:21)

R1: Daichi Hashimoto/Danshoku Dino bt Keisuke Ishii/Takayuki Ueki (9:53)

R1: Smile Yankees (HARASHIMA/Yuko Miyamoto) bt Yukio Sakaguchi/Yuya Aoki (3:28)

R1: Isami Kodaka/Yoshihisa Uto bt Masahiro Takanashi/Tatsuhiko Yoshino (6:34)

R1: Abdullah Kobayashi/Colt Cabana bt Minoru Fujita/Shunma Katsumata (4:21)

R1: Great Kojika/Tetsuya Endo bt Hideki Suzuki/Konosuke Takeshita in 1-count sudden death overtime (10:00)

R1: Hideki Suzuki/Konosuke Takeshita bt Great Kojika/Tetsuya Endo (1:38)

R2: Daisuke Sekimoto/Kazusada Higuchi bt Akito/Kazuki Hashimoto (1:52)

R2: Brahman Shu/Daisuke Sasaki bt Daichi Hashimoto/Danshoku Dino (8:09)

R2: Smile Yankees (HARASHIMA/Yuko Miyamoto) bt Isami Kodaka/Yoshihisa Uto (9:57)

R2: Brodie Hideki (Hideki Suzuki)/Jimmy Takeshita (Konosuke Takeshita) DDQ Stan Kobayashi (Abdullah Kobayashi)/Colt Butcher (Colt Cabana) (2:17)

R2 rematch: Brodie Hideki (Hideki Suzuki)/Jimmy Takeshita (Konosuke Takeshita) CO Stan Kobayashi (Abdullah Kobayashi)/Colt Butcher (Colt Cabana) by Countout (2:50)

SF: Daisuke Sekimoto/Kazusada Higuchi bt Smile Yankees (HARASHIMA/Yuko Miyamoto) (9:47)

SF: Brodie Hideki (Hideki Suzuki)/Jimmy Takeshita (Konosuke Takeshita) bt Brahman Shu/Daisuke Sasaki (7:02)

Dinosaur Takuma/Kazumi Kikuta/Kotaro Yoshino/MAO bt Dick Togo/Ryuji Ito/Sanshiro Takagi/TAKA Michinoku (13:16)

F: Hideki Suzuki/Konosuke Takeshita bt Daisuke Sekimoto/Kazusada Higuchi (12:44)

ZERO1 Happy New Year, Korakuen Hall 1/1/18 (attendance 835)

Ganseki Tanaka/Tsugutaka Sato bt Shoji Fukushima/Towa Iwasaki (11:06)

Shinjiro Otani/Yuko Miyamoto bt TARU/Yuji Hino (13:20)

ZERO1 United National Heavyweight champion Super Tiger bt Hartley Jackson, KAMIKAZE & Yoshikazu Yokoyama (9:39)

ZERO1 International Junior Heavyweight champion: Sean Guinness bt Tatsuhito Takaiwa (12:40)

Masamune/SUGI bt Ikuto Hidaka/Takuya Sugawara to win NWA International Lightweight Tag Team Title Match (12:11)

Masayuki Okamoto/Yutaka Yoshie bt Hideki Suzuki/Kohei Sato to win NWA Intercontinental Tag Team Titles (11:16)

Yusaku Obata bt Masato Tanaka to win ZERO1 World Heavyweight title (23:54)

All Japan Pro Wrestling New Year Wars 2018, Korakuen Hall, 2/1/18 (attendance 1,522)

Keiichi Sato bt Yusuke Okada (5:29)

Atsushi Maruyama/Dick Togo/Masanobu Fuchi bt Osamu Nishimura/Ultimo Dragon/Yohei Nakajima (4:39)

NEXTREAM (Kento Miyahara/Naoya Nomura/Yuma Aoyagi)/Yoshitatsu bt Hikaru Sato/KAI/Ryouji Sai/The Bodyguard (7:39)

Battle Royal: KAI bt Atsushi Maruyama, Black Tiger, Fuminori Abe, Hikaru Sato, Kaji Tomato, Keiichi Sato, Kento Miyahara, Masanobu Fuchi, Naoya Nomura, Osamu Nishimura, Ryouji Sai, The Bodyguard, Yohei Nakajima, Yoshitatsu, Yuma Aoyagi, Yusuke Okada, Yutaka Yoshie (10:48)

Violent Giants (Shuji Ishikawa/Suwama)/Atsushi Aoki defeat Burning Wild (Jun Akiyama/Takao Omori)/Koji Iwamoto (8:24)

AJPW World Junior Heavyweight champion: TAJIRI bt Kotaro Suzuki (12:42)

Triple Crown champion Joe Doering bt Zeus (20:09)

Big Japan Pro Wrestling New Year 2018, Korakuen Hall, 2/1/18 (attendance 1,568)

Masaki Morihiro/Yuya Aoki bt Takuho Kato/Takuya Nomura (12:18)

Kazuki Hashimoto/Kota Sekifuda/Tatsuhiko Yoshino bt Shinobu/Speed Of Sounds (Hercules Senga/ Tsutomu Oosugi) (7:41)

Yankee Two Kenju (Isami Kodaka/Yuko Miyamoto)/Minoru Fujita/Ryuichi Sekine bt Brahman Kei/Brahman Shu/Kankuro Hoshino/TAJIRI (9:35)

Ryota Hama/Taishi Takizawa/Yasufumi Nakanoue bt Hideyoshi Kamitani/Kazumi Kikuta/Yoshihisa Uto (11:30)

Barbed Wire Board Death Match: Abdullah Kobayashi/Jaki Numazawa/Ryuji Ito bt Masaya Takahashi/Takayuki Ueki/Toshiyuki Sakuda (9:44)

Twin Towers (Kohei Sato/Shuji Ishikawa) bt Daisuke Sekimoto/Hideki Suzuki (10:19)

BJW Strong World Heavyweight champion Daichi Hashimoto bt Ryuichi Kawakami (17:59)

Five Nails Board, Light Tubes & Cage Death Match: BJW Death Match Heavyweight champion Masashi Takeda bt Takumi Tsukamoto (17:08)

FREEDOMS Happy New Freedom 2018, Shin-Kiba 1st RING, 3/1/18 (attendance 220)

Dragon Libre bt Chikara (7:30)

King Of FREEDOM World Title Next Challenger Tournament First Round Match: Kenji Fukimoto bt Takashi Sasaki (7:48)

King Of FREEDOM World Title Next Challenger Tournament First Round Match: GENTARO bt Daisuke Masaoka (9:36)

UWA World Junior Heavyweight champion Yuya Susumu bt Kamui (11:51)

KAZMA SAKAMOTO/Mammoth Sasaki/Toru Sugiura bt Gunso/Masashi Takeda/Minoru Fujita (12:05)

Jun Kasai bt Tomoya Hirata (11:37)

King Of FREEDOM World Title Next Challenger Tournament Final Match: Kenji Fukimoto bt GENTARO (13:31)

Stardom New Years Stars 2018, Shin-Kiba 1st RING, 3/1/18 (attendance 445)

Shiki Shibusawa bt Hanan & Ruaka (5:36)

Kaori Yoneyama bt Hiromi Mimura (7:21)

Miranda/Xia Brookside bt Konami/Starlight Kid (7:16)

Kay Lee Ray/Nicole Savoy/Rachael Ellering bt Mary Apache/Team Jungle (Jungle Kyona/Natsuko Tora) (11:41)

Queen's Quest (AZM/HZK/Io Shirai/Momo Watanabe) bt Oedo Tai (Hana Kimura/Kagetsu/Kris Wolf/Natsu Sumire) (18:09)

Tokyo Joshi Pro, Korakuen Hall, 4/1/18 (attendance 1,201)

Hinano/Miu bt Hikari/Raku (8:55)

Marika Kobashi/Nodoka-Oneesan/Yuu bt Hyper Misao/Rika Tatsumi/Yuki Kamifuki (11:05)

Veda Scott bt Maho Kurone (6:55)

Danshoku Dino bt Maki Ito (12:34)

Azusa Christie/Saki-sama bt Nonoko /Yuna Manase (12:20)

Tag champions Shoko Nakajima/Yuka Sakazaki bt Mizuki/Riho (17:46)

Miyu Yamashita bt Reika Saiki to win TOKYO Princess Of Princess Title (14:58)

NJPW Wrestle Kingdom 12, Tokyo Dome, 4/1/18 (attendance 34.995 paid)

New Japan Rumble: Masahito Kakihara bt BUSHI, Chase Owens, Cheeseburger, David Finlay, Delirious, El Desperado, Gino Gambino, Hiroyoshi Tenzan, Jushin Thunder Liger, Katsuya Kitamura, Leo Tonga, Manabu Nakanishi, Satoshi Kojima, TAKA Michinoku, Tiger Mask, Toa Henare, YOSHI-HASHI, Yoshinobu Kanemaru, Yuji Nagata & Yujiro Takahashi (32:06)

Young Bucks (Matt Jackson/Nick Jackson) bt Roppongi 3K (SHO/YOH) (w/Rocky Romero) to beat IWGP Junior Heavyweight Tag Team Title (18:49)

NEVER Openweight Six Man Tag Team Title Four Way Gauntlet Match Match: CHAOS (Beretta/Tomohiro Ishii/Toru Yano) bt BULLET CLUB (Bad Luck Fale/Tama Tonga/Tanga Loa) and Suzuki-gun (Taichi/Takashi Iizuka/Zack Sabre Jr.) and War Machine (Hanson/Raymond Rowe)/Michael Elgin and Juice Robinson/Ryusuke Taguchi/Togi Makabe (17:03)

Kota Ibushi p Cody (w/Brandi Rhodes) (15:08)

Los Ingobernables de Japon (EVIL/SANADA) bt Killer Elite Squad (Davey Boy Smith Jr/Lance Archer) to win the IWGP Tag Team Titles (14:14)

Hair vs. Hair Death Match: Hirooki Goto defeats Minoru Suzuki to win the NEVER Openweight Title (18:04)

Will Ospreay bt IWGP Junior Heavyweight champion Marty Scurll, Hiromu Takahashi & KUSHIDA to win title (21:18)

IWGP Intercontinental champion Hiroshi Tanahashi bt Jay White (19:43)

No DQ: IWGP United States Heavyweight champion Kenny Omega bt Chris Jericho (34:36)

IWGP Heavyweight champion Kazuchika Okada (w/Gedo) p Tetsuya Naito (34:26)

DDT D-King Grand Prix 2018, Shinjuku Face, 5/1/18 (attendance 464)

Joey Ryan/Veda Scott bt New Wrestling Aidoru (Makoto Oishi/Shunma Katsumata), Antonio Honda/Soma Takao & KUDO & Toru Owashi (8:44)

D-Ou Grand Prix 2018 Block B Match: Yukio Sakaguchi bt Kazusada Higuchi (7:48)

D-Ou Grand Prix 2018 Block A Match: Tetsuya Endo bt Masahiro Takanashi (6:01)

D-Ou Grand Prix 2018 Block B Match: Akito bt Daisuke Sasaki (12:03)

D-Ou Grand Prix 2018 Block A Match: Keisuke Ishii bt HARASHIMA (12:45)

D-Ou Grand Prix 2018 Block B Match: Shuji Ishikawa bt Mike Bailey (15:15)

D-Ou Grand Prix 2018 Block A Match: Jiro Kuroshio bt Konosuke Takeshita (23:23)

28760302R00044

Printed in Great Britain
by Amazon